THE SIX SIGMA BOOK
FOR HEALTHCARE

THE SIX SIGMA BOOK FOR HEALTHCARE

Improving Outcomes by Reducing Errors

Robert Barry
Amy Murcko
Clifford Brubaker

Health Administration Press

ACHE Management Series

Your board, staff, or clients may also benefit from this book's insight. For more information on quantity discounts, contact the Health Administration Press Marketing Manager at (312) 424-9470.

Sixth Printing 2009

Library of Congress Cataloging-in-Publication Data

Barry, Robert.
   The six sigma book for healthcare : improving outcomes by reducing errors /
authors, Robert Barry, Amy Murcko, Clifford Brubaker.
      p.   cm.
   Includes bibliographical references.
   ISBN 1-56793-191-X (alk. paper)
   1. Medical errors—Prevention.   2. Six Sigma (Quality control standard)   3. Health facilities—Risk management.   4. Quality control.   I. Murcko, Amy.   II. Brubaker, Cliff.   III. Title.
R729.8 .B37   2002
362.1—dc21
                                          2002068760

The paper used in this publication meets the minimum requirements of American National Standard for Information Sciences—Permanence of Paper for Printed Library Materials, ANSI Z39.48–1984. ∞™

Acquisitions editor: Marcy McKay; Project manager: Joyce Sherman; Text designer: Matt Avery; Cover designer: Greg Moore

Health Administration Press
A division of the Foundation of the
   American College of Healthcare Executives
1 North Franklin Street, Suite 1700
Chicago, IL 60606-3491
(312) 424-2800

Table of Contents

Foreword

The history of healthcare in the United States since the end of World War II has been shaped by four basic concepts: access, cost, quality, and equity. Each of these has appeared sequentially in the postwar period, and each continues to compete for prominence on the national policy agenda and in the operational priorities of the nation's healthcare institutions. As one of these four central themes, the search for enhancements in clinical quality and efficiency has been a prominent element of the national healthcare environment for more than a quarter-century.

Access, particularly for those with fewer resources, was supported through the Hill-Burton Act, the legislation that helped hospitals expand their capacity, supported the development and expansion of community health centers, provided subsidized health insurance for the elderly (Medicare), and supported states in their efforts to provide care to the indigent through the Medicaid program.

In one of the most startling examples of legislative effectiveness, all of these initiatives led to an expansion of healthcare services and an increased number of clinicians and facilities, and they also contributed to healthcare's increasing share of the gross national product. Alarmed by this growth, legislators initiated a series of efforts to restrain expenditures. The most notable of these efforts were the Medicare Prospective Payment System of the early 1980s and the current Balanced Budget Act, which subsidized an important national fiscal objective through reductions in Medicare payments.

Even as policy directions and parallel pressures from private payers drove down reimbursements for medical services, hospitals and clinicians discovered that the best medical care is always the least expensive, although the reverse is not always the case. This helped stimulate a series of movements within healthcare to measure, improve, and report on clinical outcomes.

For many of us facing the challenges of managing healthcare facilities during the last quarter of the twentieth century, our first introduction to the principles of quality improvement came from learning about quality circles. These circles were borrowed from Japanese industries, and they taught us about the benefits of group efforts to analyze and improve work processes. Later, we were shown the economic principles of quality improvement through Crosby's *Quality is Free,* a short introduction to the principle that, although quality is available at no cost, a lack of quality is extremely expensive because of rework, duplication, and human suffering. Most of us, armed with Crosby's diminutive paperback, convened work groups at our hospitals to identify wasted efforts and manmade errors and to design approaches to correcting them. At the same time, we expanded our reading lists to include Deming and Juran so that we might acquire the technical skills of total quality management or continuous quality improvement.

A major catalyst for our learning was Dr. Don Berwick, a Harvard pediatrician whose genius guided him to develop the Institute for Healthcare Improvement, the annual meeting of which was a requirement for anyone serious about applying the principles of continuous quality improvement to healthcare. The Institute became one of the nation's largest learning collaboratives, and it led to a grid of personal networks through which initiatives were developed, tested, and shared. Our planning skills were sharpened through the Hoshin processes, and recognition was provided by the Baldrige awards for excellence in quality enhancement.

All of our learning was not without challenges, however. We discovered that bringing changes to the nonclinical arenas of healthcare was easy compared to changing the clinical areas, so we shortened the waiting time for patients to be admitted to a floor, reduced billing errors, and got the correct meal to the patient more frequently than before. However, nurturing similar achievements in the world of clinical services, particularly those provided by voluntary, community-based physicians, was difficult. The continuous quality improvement concepts assume collaborative decision making, teamwork across several levels of a hierarchy, and the sharing of data; none of these concepts typify the realm of private physician practice.

Today, however, the world of healthcare looks different, and this is in part because of several important new trends. One of these is the emphasis placed on quality measures and improvements by the Joint Commission for Accreditation of Health Care Organizations, which requires the reporting of sentinel events (major actual or possible clinical errors) and encourages the use of root-cause analysis to identify the causes of systemic error and to build permanent corrections. Another is the publication of two successive studies by the national Institute of Medicine. The first, *To Err is Human*, presented a somewhat alarmist view of the frequency and human effect of medical errors. The second, *Crossing the Chasm*, provided a more reason-based approach to error reduction through formal processes of continuous clinical quality improvement.

The need for quality improvement is now clear. With a demand for the reduction of errors and a parallel need to reduce costs in an effort to adapt to declining reimbursements, hospitals and healthcare organizations have focused on enhancements in both operational and clinical improvements, and they have actively sought techniques to guide these enhancements. Clinicians, led by heroes in the field such as Intermountain Health Care's Dr. Brent James, have discovered the science in quality management, and they have joined the parade toward continuing improvement.

Although the emphasis on error reduction has a negative connotation, the issue has raised consciousness and energized the medical community to seek solutions that have an effect in the broader context of quality improvement. In one community, a broad effort sponsored by a coalition of businesses, insurers, foundations, and healthcare providers has given rise to the Pittsburgh Regional Healthcare Initiative, which seeks to apply the principles of the Toyota Production System to healthcare to improve clinical outcomes throughout the community. This effort has been one of several that have borrowed industrial models and applied them to healthcare.

As hospitals and clinicians join together to create an improved field of service, they seek models that have proven their efficacy and that can be applied to healthcare efficiently. The combination of need, motivation, and resources is presented with great clarity in this book, which introduces the Six Sigma approach to error reduction in healthcare. Six Sigma, which provides a formal analysis of the sources of error and establishes a high standard for acceptable quality, has been shown in an industrial setting to be a powerful tool for quality improvement; it has begun to be broadly accepted in healthcare as well. The benefit of this book is that it demystifies this approach and provides the technical knowledge necessary to begin to apply the Six Sigma principles. It now remains for us only to learn these principles, to allow them to build on our knowledge base of improvement techniques, and to apply them in an unremitting commitment to a new ideal of healthcare quality.

The principles of Six Sigma have the capacity to help those of us in healthcare to address the primary issues of the postwar world; costs will be reduced through greater clinical efficacy, and with reduced costs, enhancing access may be feasible, particularly for the nation's 44 million uninsured. With increased access, the challenges of equity as reflected by significant disparities in health status by gender, race, and income may also be addressed.

The goals of Six Sigma are relatively simple: to ensure that all of us who access health services will be guaranteed appropriate, timely, and error-free care. With these enhancements, the limited resources of our healthcare system may be extended to more people who need them.

Ian G. Rawson, Ph.D., CHE
President of the Hospital Council of Western Pennsylvania

Preface

We have collaborated on this book because we believe that healthcare executives are open to new management methods that offer the prospect of improving healthcare. Six Sigma sets about eliminating error. The book explains how it works. We address each matter from the management perspective. This book deals only with healthcare, a field in which, even today, the patient remains literally in the hands of caregivers.

The book is jargon-free, and there are no new acronyms to puzzle over. A few odd-looking words appear that may be new, so the reader's vocabulary will be enriched just a little. Most of the concepts of Six Sigma are common sense, and this will be clear as you become more familiar with them.

Someone wrote that poetry reminded him of things he didn't know he knew. Six Sigma does that, too.

Robert Barry, Ph.D.
Amy Murcko, APRN
Clifford Brubaker, Ph.D.

Acknowledgments

We are pleased to express our appreciation in acknowledgment of the contributions of Matthew R. Barry, Ph.D., of Houston, Texas, for his many helpful discussions and his corrections to the text and to Thomas Murcko, Six Sigma Black Belt, of Hermitage, Pennsylvania, for his assistance with the cases.

PART I

Introduction

Six Sigma is for those healthcare organization managers who believe that eliminating defects and errors is good for patients, good for the community, and good for management and employees alike.

The Six Sigma Standard:

3.4 errors per million opportunities for error

Six Sigma is a management method that moves the organization in an orderly way from its present error rate to a very low error rate, with the specific target being 3.4 errors per million opportunities.

Six Sigma arose in the high-tech industrial sector, but leading hospitals are now applying Six Sigma to their own operations (Miller, Desmarais, and Calvaruso 2001), and more healthcare applications can be expected to follow.

Although the point of eliminating error is not necessarily to save money, studies (e.g., McKee 2002) show that the cost borne by the healthcare system just to treat patients for injuries done to the patient by the system is substantial. Seven percent of hospital inpatients are victims of drug-related errors alone, with an average cost of care of $5,000 per case. Add liability and litigation costs and the costs of resources made nonproductive by errors causing delays in service, and the total cost of error in healthcare is very likely to be more than 10 percent of the total system cost. That is a lot of money, and it is a lot of imperfect service. Everyone wants the healthcare system to do better. The Institute of Medicine has renewed its call for systematic improvement. Indeed, all professional and institutional organizations are calling for improvement.

Six Sigma can help. The Six Sigma method is acquired by training, and the principles are quite simple and direct.

This book addresses the Six Sigma methods for the following:
1. Error prevention
2. Problem solving
3. Problem detection
4. Change management

It would be nice to think that the application of error prevention would be enough and that this would eliminate errors. Unfortunately, even Six Sigma cannot get the error rate down to zero. Furthermore, if the organization already exists, it has legacy issues to deal with and problems to be solved. Change, whether desired or not, is inevitable and must be managed. Operations need to be tracked over a long period of time so that problems will be detected at an early stage. Fortuitously, the four topics this book addresses come as package. Indeed, most organizations find themselves first applying the problem-solving methods because they have a problem that management wants solved. When a solution presents itself, it will include error-prevention methods, and it will require some change to be implemented, so the change management methods are applied. Following this, the change is tracked over the long term, and the problem detection methods are applied. The desired outcome is an organization applying the most modern methods to drive the error rate further and further down.

The Six Sigma problem-solving methods can be applied to address sentinel events as defined by the Joint Commission on the Accreditation of Healthcare Organizations.

Most organizations that take up Six Sigma choose to train a small number of their own people to apply Six Sigma; this is more economical than hiring long-term consultants. Trained Six Sigma personnel are called "green belts" if they are qualified to carry out projects and "black belts" if they are qualified to design projects. Master black belts hold the highest rank and are qualified to teach Six Sigma to others and to direct multiple projects under management direction. Some major corporations that have found success with Six Sigma now require all management candidates to be qualified to at least the Six Sigma green belt level. However, that is not necessary to get the process started; a small nucleus of trained Six Sigma personnel is sufficient for getting started.

This book is written for a general audience, with healthcare managers and practitioners in mind. No particular math skills are required, nor is a background knowledge of statistics. The book and cases can be used as a text for training green belt and black belt candidates under the leadership of a Six Sigma trainer; the cases are graded for green belt and black belt study. The general audience may wish to work out the same cases for their own benefit and amusement.

Some readers will expect a Six Sigma book to have mathematical formulae because the title sounds mathematical; those readers will find a page of very nice formulae in the appendix. Other readers may ignore that appendix, comforted with the knowledge that no higher math skills are needed to follow the book or to carry out Six Sigma projects.

An annotated bibliography appears in the back of this book. The reader may find the annotations somewhat helpful in deciding which of the titles merit closer inspection. A glossary of terms is also included.

The web site that accompanies this book, www.ache.org/pubs/barry/ start.cfm, includes all of the data for the cases, sample cases that have been worked out, report templates, and additional details on some examples in the text. Because working the cases requires the use of a spreadsheet program (such as Microsoft Excel®), an "ice breaker" spreadsheet is also included to help novices get started.

Six Sigma:
Why, What, How?

Six Sigma management methods set quantitative error rate objectives because experience has shown that, lacking specific goals, improvement is too slow and unsatisfactory for the needs of the day.

Six Sigma is a management method that addresses error prevention, problem solving, problem detection, and managed change.

Six Sigma uses a collection of management practices to achieve its specified goal. Some of these practices are based on statistics, but many are not.

WHY SIX SIGMA?

You are a healthcare executive, or you expect to be one in due course. Your organization provides error-free care to your patients, your patients are discharged on schedule every time, every patient leaves with a correct financial statement and the proper instructions on at-home care, and you surely have attained peace of mind with regard to the management of your organization. Your facility has happy and loyal clientele, your staff has professional satisfaction, and your managers and resources are applied to positive purposes. If this describes your situation, you can close the book now with our congratulations.

If you have not quite reached that level of perfection but errors at your organization are exceedingly rare, you, too, can close the book now with our congratulations.

If you are still reading, this book may be what you've been looking for. You are committed voluntarily to the standards of the Joint Commission on Accreditation of Health Care Organizations (Joint Commission), including their standards for sentinel events (events that are life-threatening or worse and for which a root-cause analysis and system rectification plan are required). Six Sigma provides a systematic method for doing the analysis and rectifying the system.

You are committed to the Joint Commission standards for performance improvement. Six Sigma provides a systematic method for quantifying the existing system, defining trials, measuring progress, and characterizing long-term conformance.

You probably have a total quality management program, a continuous quality improvement program, and a quality assurance program, and you conform to the standard practices of each of your health professions. You undertook all of these as means to an end: error-free provision of healthcare services.

You know instinctively the following:

- An organization that never makes errors has happy and loyal clientele.
- An organization that never makes errors is easy to manage.
- An organization that never makes errors has positive uses for resources.
- An organization that never makes errors attracts the best candidates for employment.
- An organization that never makes errors has peace of mind in the executive suite.

Frank Gilbreth, the efficiency expert, broke tasks down into small elements such as grasp, lift, twist. He called these *therbligs*, derived from Gilbreth spelled backwards.

Gilbreth was played by Clifton Webb in the movie *Cheaper by the Dozen*.

You also know that untoward events can happen, even in the best of organizations; therefore, you would wish to have at hand an organized management method for dealing with such events. Six Sigma provides such a method as it may be applied to products and services.

Efforts to improve production processes started in a systematic way before World War I with Taylor (1911), Gilbreth (1894), and others, who were known as efficiency experts. After World War I, a theory was developed that allowed the benefits to be applied systematically to all kinds of production. The best known work was done by the telephone company at Bell Labs and in AT&T's manufacturing arm, known in those days as Western Electric. Other major companies did similar work; the AT&T

work is best known because, having no competitors, AT&T did not mind publishing its findings. This body of work came to be called "scientific management."

Then came World War II. For three years, the American War Production Board ran the biggest command economy in the history of the world. Much of the production was done by giant companies that already knew scientific management, but much was also done by others who had been running small companies and who suddenly found themselves employing thousands of workers. They needed help. The War Production Board saw to it that they got that help by mandating scientific management across the board. The results impressed our enemies and our allies alike as war materiel flowed from factories deprived of the 15 million men then in uniform and staffed instead by women, youngsters, oldsters, and just about everyone else who was available, few of whom had ever seen the inside of a factory before.

After the war, things returned to normal in the United States, with pent-up consumer demand replacing military demand in most industries. Without the War Production Board to tell them how to manage their work, some companies continued to apply scientific management, and some did not. With demand so high, not much discipline came from the marketplace to force manufacturers to perform well.

Meanwhile, General Douglas MacArthur saw the need to revive Japanese industry to get the its postwar economy going. The American market for manufactured goods was, relatively speaking, open to imports. Exporting to the United States would earn Japan some hard currency. Adding technology in the form of scientific management would speed things up, so MacArthur engaged a group of production experts from the United States to advise Japanese industrialists on how to manage production. Among these were two Americans who figure prominently in the story: C. Edwards Deming (Walton 1990) and Joseph M. Juran (Juran 1995). Both enjoyed long professional lives and advised Japanese clients for decades while maintaining their American practices.

At the time, Japan had two big hurdles to overcome to implement a successful export strategy: the county had no money, and it was a long way from the American market. Because of the lack of money, each raw material item was precious, and nothing could be wasted. Because of their distance from the American market, the Japanese manufacturers had to ship a product that would satisfy the American customer

1. Create consistency of purpose.
2. Adopt the new philosophy.
3. Cease dependence on inspection.
4. End the practice of awarding business on the basis of price alone.
5. Improve constantly.
6. Institute training/retraining on the job.
7. Institute leadership for system improvement.
8. Drive out fear.
9. Break down barriers between departments.
10. Eliminate arbitrary quotas and slogans without providing resources.
11. Eliminate work standards (quotas) for management.
12. Remove barriers to pride of workmanship.
13. Institute education and self-improvement for everyone.
14. Transform everyone's job to transform the organization.

immediately on delivery because goods could not be shipped back to the factory to fix mistakes.

In short, the postwar Japanese had to build the product right with no waste or else their strategy would fail. Inspired by clear thinking on the matter and lacking any alternative, the Japanese export companies bore down and applied everything they could learn about low-error, low-loss manufacturing methods. They absorbed everything Deming and Juran had to offer, and they applied what they learned with zeal.

The Japanese started with transistor radios and motor scooters and moved over time to automobiles, sophisticated consumer products, and capital goods, staying with the manufacturing discipline well after they had plenty of hard currency in the bank. They were discovering that their quality reputation earned them market share while minimizing costs.

This brings us up to the 1970s, which was a time of turmoil, stagflation, and malaise in the United States. American production was in such disarray that these popular-literature business theories emerged:

- Murphy's Law (Murphy 1949)—Anything that can go wrong will go wrong

- Parkinson's Law (Parkinson 1957)—Work expands to fill the time available
- the Peter Principle (Peter 1979)—Managers are promoted to their level of incompetence

American companies lost market share at home and abroad. The American government tried to help by imposing guidance in the form of quality assurance requirements on various civilian industries. These became institutionalized—that is, bureaucratized—over time, and they may or may not have been very helpful. American industrialists then trooped to Japan to learn from the quality masters.

In the 1980s, manufacturing started to turn around in the United States. Philip Crosby, head of quality assurance for the then-huge ITT corporation, published a best-seller called *Quality is Free* (Crosby 1979). Crosby observed (and it was confirmed by a great number of industries) that American companies were spending 20 percent of their time, capital, and management resources fixing things. If a fraction of that effort was put into doing something right in the first place, the company would recoup a lot of time and money.

Business rediscovered Deming and Juran. The *In Search of Excellence* books (Peters and Waterman 1982) sold by the carload. Companies signed up for total quality management and later for continuous quality improvement programs.

The American government created the Malcolm Baldrige Award to recognize efforts in the improvement of quality. The government later added a separate Malcolm Baldrige award for healthcare (National Institute of Standards and Technology 2001). The International Standards Organization recognized quality assurance by issuing the ISO 9000 family of standards.

By 1990, American manufacturing companies were generally competent at producing quality goods and were holding their own. That did not, however, prove to be the end of the story. Motorola was the first to say that not enough progress was being made and that something more had to be done. If not, the quality level would never get to the standard they felt they *had* to meet to compete in their markets against very serious international competition. Motorola instituted the first Six Sigma program. Other major companies, most notably General Electric, IBM, and Texas Instruments, followed. These were followed in turn, curiously enough, by the Japanese company Sony. Transaction-oriented service companies

Crosby's 14 Points

1. Management commitment
2. Quality improvement team
3. Quality measurement
4. Cost of quality evaluation
5. Quality awareness
6. Corrective action
7. Ad-hoc committee for zero-defect planning
8. Supervisory training
9. Zero defects day
10. Goal setting
11. Error-cause removal
12. Recognition
13. Quality councils
14. Do it over again

such as American Express also took up Six Sigma practices; many banks are now following American Express' lead.

These companies had not been asleep between World War I and 1990; they had been leaders every step along the way. (Despite its recent downturn, Motorola maintains superior engineering capabilities.) They had quality assurance programs, total quality management programs, and continuous quality improvement programs. They knew everything that could be known about scientific management. They were, as they had always been, leaders in production management.

So why did they decide they needed something new? Something more?

These leaders came to believe that maintaining their good management practices would result in products with a few defects per 1,000. They wanted not to get to zero defects, because that would be impossible, but to a few defects per *million*; that is a thousand times better than what they had been doing, and they felt they had to get to that level. On the basis of their experience, they realized that their existing programs would take a very long time—too long—to get where they wanted to be, and they did not have much time. They needed to take action.

Thus, Six Sigma. Six Sigma goes beyond "continuous improvement" programs to specific, numeric goals. These goals have now been shown to be attainable in many industries.

The Japanese experience is helpful because, in one human-generation, postwar Japanese industry went through four complete technology-generations, from handwork to hand-fed machines to self-feeding machines to self-feeding and self-monitoring machines. Most Japanese manufacturing was done in small batches, so special attention was paid to reducing set-up time and understanding the flow of work.

Where is healthcare today? We are still doing a lot of handwork. Some mechanization and computerization of instrumentation has arrived, and some robots are used, for example, in hip surgery. More mechanization is probably coming, but right now healthcare is largely handwork.

The contributions made back in the handwork stage of industrialization reduced back-breaking physical effort, organized the work and the tool crib, designed new tools, broke down tasks so they could be improved step by step, and taught workers to inspect their own work.

Many of these improvements were made specifically to reduce the frequency of worker error. With some thought, those lessons learned can today be applied to healthcare.

WHAT IS SIX SIGMA?

Six Sigma is a systematic method for improving the output of the organization by improving the quality of the system. This is done by preventing error, solving problems, managing change, and monitoring long-term performance in quantitative terms so that any incipient problems are detected before they become bothersome. It is a quantitative method that deals with measures commonly called "quality measures." Before discussing the application of a quality measure, having a definition of *quality* will be helpful.

The Four Facets of Six Sigma

1. Preventing error
2. Solving problems
3. Detecting problems
4. Managing change

The Institute of Medicine (IOM 2001) defines quality as "the degree to which health services for individuals and populations increase the likelihood of desired health outcomes and are consistent with current professional knowledge." This goes in a good direction and would be hard to contradict, but it does not apply to something that can be quantified.

Crosby (1979) provided an operable definition of quality by saying, "Quality is conformance to requirements." Nothing more, nothing less. This is a functional measure, and it works with something that can be quantified. Does the work meet the requirements or not? Does it pass or fail? What is the percentage of passes and the percentage of failures? No credit is given for being close or for good intentions; there is no extra credit for doing more than the specification required.

If the Crosby meaning of quality applies, what, then, is an error? To be consistent with Crosby, an error must be that which reduces conformance to requirements. An error need not, by itself, cause conformance to fail; an error need only detract.

Error in Healthcare

In industry, a defective part is reworked or tossed in the reject pile. In healthcare, there is no reject pile, so any error causes rework, and rework takes time and resources.

Errors in healthcare service include the following:

- Administrative error in admission
- Incorrect or untimely diagnosis
- Error in medication

- Error in therapy or other treatment
- Administrative error in the patient record
- Untimely treatment
- Departure from nursing standard
- Departure from any other professional standard
- Error in prerelease patient indoctrination
- Administrative error in discharge
- Error in any financial statement
- Error in take-home instructions or medication
- Delayed discharge
- Other such action or inaction that has an effect on the timely treatment and discharge of the patient

Errors include direct injuries to the patient and all of the other things that detract from timely and effective treatment: a patient falls in the bathroom; an immobile patient is not turned in bed and risks pressure ulcers; x-rays are misfiled; supplies run out; schedules are botched; a department runs out of nurses and has to oblige some nurses to work a double shift; one department smooths out its work load by bunching the work up in the next department; billing errors are made. All these possibilities and many more detract from the organization's service to the patient and community.

Plenty of other management issues are not directly involved in service: unauthorized people parking in the doctors' parking slots; the capital budget campaign; noisy helicopters annoying the neighbors; succession planning; recruiting. Six Sigma has nothing to offer for these; it addresses the delivery of services only.

Six Sigma and Quality Management Programs

Baldrige Award for Health Care

Looking at the year 2001 criteria set forth for the Malcolm Baldrige Health Care Award is instructive (National Institute of Standards and Technology 2001). The Baldrige Award is the pinnacle of management-for-quality attainment, and it is highly sought. Award winners are to be commended for their attainment and can be expected to call attention to themselves at every opportunity. Who would not?

Here are the Baldrige goals for 2001:

- Delivery of ever-improving value to patients and other customers and contributing to improved healthcare quality
- Improvement of overall organizational effectiveness and capabilities as a healthcare provider
- Organizational and personal learning

The 2001 Baldrige criteria, which provide a structured way of meeting the Baldrige goals, are listed below in the left column. The corresponding Six Sigma element is marked in the right column.

FIGURE 1: BALDRIGE AWARD CRITERIA AND RELATED SIX SIGMA ELEMENTS

2001 Baldrige Criteria	Six Sigma
Leadership	
Strategic planning	
Focus on patients, other customers, and markets	
Information and analysis	
Staff focus	
Process management	
Organizational performance results	3.4 errors per million opportunities

The Baldrige criteria are seven useful, important, and significant measures of an organization. Six Sigma includes only one such measure: the error rate.

Total Quality Management

A similar comparison with total quality management may be helpful. The philosophy of total quality management (Hansen 2001) is given in the left column of Figure 2 below, with corresponding Six Sigma criteria in the right column.

Total Quality Management	Six Sigma
Collective responsibilities	
Managerial leadership	
Accountability	
Participation	
Performance and process expectations	
Flexible planning	
Benchmarking	
Concurrent performance appraisal	
Continuous improvement	3.4 errors per million opportunities

This total quality management list compares rather closely with the Baldrige list above, and both are commendable lists. Note that in this case as well the Six Sigma list is short, with only one entry. For completeness, note that although total quality management is derived from the Deming model, some divergence in view has been seen: Deming was utterly opposed to any performance appraisals, concurrent or otherwise. Similar comparisons could be made with iso 9000 and continuous quality improvement characteristics versus those of the Six Sigma model. The same conclusion would be reached.

The essence of the comparisons is this: total quality management, the Baldrige characteristics, continuous quality improvement, and iso 9000 are all based on the premise that getting the *process* right will eventually lead to getting the *output* right, with no time scale mentioned. Six Sigma focuses on getting the output right, starting right now. Moreover, nothing in total quality management, continuous quality improvement, or iso 9000 precludes the application of Six Sigma. Indeed, Six Sigma complements such process-oriented policies.

Six Sigma responds directly to the Joint Commission requirements for sentinel events and root-cause analysis; these will be addressed in a later chapter.

HOW IS SIX SIGMA APPLIED?

Mature Six Sigma organizations simply include Six Sigma methods in everything they do, so no special attention is required. Before getting to be that mature, organizations select projects for Six Sigma attention, execute those projects, measure results, and then take up more projects.

A Six Sigma project addresses work to be redesigned, a problem to be solved, a change to be instituted, or a key process or set of processes to be monitored so that any problem can be detected and resolved. Usually these three are connected; once a problem is solved, some change will be instituted to provide the solution, and the new process will be monitored over the long term to detect any new problems. Six Sigma error prevention techniques will be implemented in the design of the solution to the problem.

Six Sigma projects are designed by black belts, who also oversee the projects. The projects are normally carried out by green belts. For early projects and major projects, the organization will assign a senior manager to act as a sponsor.

Some organizations have Six Sigma champions who promote Six Sigma; whether that is a good idea depends on the organization's culture. If the organization relies on the line organization to manage new methods, no particular need exists to also have champions. If the organization likes matrix management methods, champions may well fit in and accelerate the inculcation of Six Sigma into the organization as a whole.

To start, an organization needs two or three black belts and a few green belts. Theoretically, one black belt would be enough, but one is a fragile number. Black belts are members of the organization who have an interest and are willing to accept training in something new; they do not have to have an advanced math background. Training can be done on-site or at a training facility, preferably by a Six Sigma training firm that specializes in healthcare.

In the long run, the organization may want to have about 1 percent of the professional staff trained at the black belt level and about 4 or 5 percent trained as green belts.

A typical on-site training program runs for a week, with the trainees taken away from their regular duties for essentially all of that week. By the end of that week, each will have been assigned a training project to do during the balance of the month. The trainer will be on call during that month to coach the trainees as necessary. The group meets again

Six Sigma Belts

- Green belts can carry out projects.
- Black belts can design and direct projects.
- Master black belts can train others and direct multiple projects.

General Electric's Six Sigma Program

GE has embraced Six Sigma throughout the giant corporation, requiring all management candidates to be at least green belts. The company has an informative web site about this: www.ge.com/ sixsigma for one or two days to review the projects, straighten out any difficulties, and award green belts to successful participants.

Trainees pursuing the black belt will repeat the process, with another week of additional classroom training followed by a more substantial project that typically runs for another month. At the end of that second month, successful participants will be awarded the black belt.

Black belts who take a keen interest may wish to pursue the master black belt at a training facility or through an online training company. Master black belts need more of a mathematical background or experience in statistical analysis as well as an interest in teaching others.

Many companies provide Six Sigma training, although few have specialized in healthcare issues. Most do industrial training, with an emphasis on factory performance. Many Six Sigma consulting companies will perform Six Sigma projects on a fee basis; some do both training and consulting. Relatively few have consulting experience in healthcare, although the number is growing.

This book includes a large number of healthcare cases, in part because healthcare training material is not available to any extent elsewhere. The 20 cases in this book provide sufficient case-study material for training green belts and black belts.

Most Six Sigma training companies and consulting companies have web sites; any standard web search engine will identify them. Interested organizations may also contact the authors for training and consultation with specialization in healthcare.

Error Prevention

Errors are prevented by having the right equipment, the right infrastructure, trained personnel, and work tasks that lend themselves to being done correctly.

Errors are also prevented by managing the flow of work through the organization so that individual units are not overwhelmed by surges in demand. Hospital workflow has been getting attention recently with regard to both improving resource utilization and improving patient satisfaction (Mango and Shapiro 2001). Our attention is focused on understanding workflow principles to reduce the opportunity for error, which complements both resource utilization and patient satisfaction.

POKA-YOKE

Stopping Errors before They Happen

Poka-yoke (Shingo 1981), pronounced po' kah yo' kay, is the Japanese term for mistake-proofing. The Japanese name has caught on because it has a better ring to it than the traditional American terms (fool-proofing, idiot-proofing, and the like), all of which are pejorative. Poka-yoke, being inscrutable, carries no negative connotation.

Poka-yoke is the fruit of a hundred years' study of the design of jobs and tasks. The results are these few guidelines, which are the essence of poka-yoke:

1. Make it easier for the person to do the right thing than the wrong thing.
2. Make mistakes obvious to the person immediately so that some correction can be made on the spot.

Poka-Yoke

"Poka-yoke" translates to "prevention of error by inadvertent action."

The older Japanese term was "baka-yoke," which translates to "prevention of foolish action."

3. Allow the person to take corrective action or stop the flow before any irreversible step occurs.

Poka-yoke can also be seen as a systematic reduction of worker stress. Thinking that reduction of worker stress will mean a reduction in the worker's error rate is not rash. Getting this to work is not trivial, although the guidelines are quite simple. Take, for example, childproof caps for pill bottles. Their purpose is noble and fits exactly with the concepts of poka-yoke: they make it easier for the person in question (the child) to do the right thing (stay out of the pill bottle) than the wrong thing (get into the pill bottle). The difficulty arises in finding some cap design that keeps children out while still allowing adults to get to the pills. Because no single design for childproof caps exists, the adult wishing to open a new bottle must first figure out how this particular cap is supposed to work. Some are baffling; others require the adult to push down on the cap while turning it, which invites spilling the pills onto the floor or into the sink. The upshot may be that the bottle, once opened, is left open, which defeats the whole childproofing purpose.

Childproof caps are designed by very clever people working with unlimited budgets. Even so, the state of the art is wanting. This is offered as a cautionary tale and demonstrates that poka-yoke is not yet a settled practice of instant solutions.

Using terms like "design of work tasks" conveys the notion that, once a task is suitably designed, the matter is settled. This rarely happens, because things continue to change. Although most changes are incremental and the employee can make simple accommodations, measuring performance over time is a good practice so that any negative features that creep in are detected and dealt with in a timely manner, which is to say, before they get to be serious.

Verbal Orders

Much of medical practice relies on verbal orders, commonly from doctor to nurse. Sometimes, the doctor misspeaks; sometimes, the nurse misunderstands.

If immediate feedback is given, the second poka-yoke guideline takes effect because the error is then obvious to the order giver. If the surgeon says "scalpel" and the nurse hands over forceps, immediate, tangible feedback is given. The error gets corrected right away, and no harm is done other than a slight delay. Note that the same corrective mechanism works even if the surgeon *thinks* "scalpel" but misspeaks and says "forceps." Whichever party makes the goof, the system makes the error obvious and easy to correct on the spot. Good poka-yoke.

Now, if the situation is different and does not provide immediate feedback, poka-yoke is not being followed and trouble may lurk. Suppose the physician says "Drug A" and the nurse hears "Drug B." Or, the physician thinks "Drug A" but says "Drug B." No feedback results, and the error could go undetected for too long a time.

Many organizations outside of healthcare run on verbal orders. The navies of the world have a way of generating feedback in exactly this situation. The captain gives an order to the lieutenant, who immediately repeats it, providing the necessary feedback to make poka-yoke work. Indeed, the navy order is repeated over and over again as the order passes down the chain of command. Then the response comes back up the chain of command, repeated several times. This is done even if the officers are standing side by side.

Curiously, neither the U.S. Army nor the U.S. Air Force follow this practice. Should they?

TOPICS IN HEALTHCARE ERROR PREVENTION

Here we will consider the poka-yoke principles as they apply to topics germane to healthcare organizations.

Personalization

Wal-Mart has great big stores. Sam Walton, the founder of Wal-Mart, decided that shoppers were finding his stores too impersonal. Because shoppers have other choices, Walton wanted to encourage shoppers to use his stores rather than those of others, so he worked to take the impersonal edge off. He hired people to stand at the door and greet shoppers as they came in, hand them shopping carts, offer a big smile (the Japanese version is to have employees stand at the door and bow deeply as customers come into the store; Americans smile better than we bow), and generally be personable. The point was to make the shopper feel welcome, to personalize an impersonal experience, and to take a little stress out of the situation.

Poka-Yoke Guidelines

To eliminate error:

1. Make doing the task right easier than doing it wrong.
2. Make errors immediately obvious.
3. Make the correction of errors on the spot possible.

Many healthcare organizations appear to be going the other way. Common practice today seems to be to have the patient interact with a clipboard: sign in here, mark the time, take a seat. This is now observed in general practices, in expensive specialists' offices, and in units within hospitals. This first interaction with the patient, who is already under some degree of stress, conveys the notion that the patient is not worth any personal attention. If the patient has questions great or small (Did I park in the right lot?), they are not important enough to merit attention. The patient is told to take a seat and wait.

Would Sam Walton run a medical service this way? Because the labor cost savings is obviously trivial, the patient gets the immediate impression that the organization thinks it is not getting a satisfactory amount of insurance money and is cutting corners by firing the receptionist. If you are the patient, you think the doctor is mad at you even before you get in the door. The patient may begin to think, if the organization is cutting corners in the reception area, where else are corners being cut?

Instead of taking stress out of the situation the way Wal-Mart does, these healthcare organizations are increasing the stress on the patient. This does not decrease the likelihood of error: it surely increases it. This is distinctly not poka-yoke.

Buildings

Hospitals are trying to find ways for their big buildings to interact with patients and visitors; some are using language-free signs. For our diverse society, this is a very good idea. Symbols, once understood, are easy to recognize and interpret, even if the symbols are complex or abstract; the difficulty is figuring out what they mean the first time. Airlines have the same issue, and they deal with it by providing pamphlets in several languages to explain what the symbols mean.

Effective signage follows the first poka-yoke guideline by making it easier to get to the target destination on the first try. If taking the second poka-yoke guideline to heart, signs should also be placed where those who have wandered off the path will see them and discover immediately that they missed a turn. Following the third poka-yoke guideline allows the wanderer to correct the navigation error and get back on track.

Training for the Exceptional Event

Emerson (1860) wrote, "A great part of courage is the courage of having done the thing before." One hopes that healthcare workers do not need to call upon their courage very often, but the thought does extend to dealing with exceptional events. If the worker has dealt with the same event before, he or she is more likely to do the right thing. Being prepared makes doing the right thing easier, which very much complies with poka-yoke.

Airline pilots train for exceptional events with the use of flight simulators, which can create all manner of exceptional situations for the pilot to handle. The simulators are multimillion dollar investments, the training time is extensive and recurring, and simulator staff salary is expensive. Those of us who fly from time to time are happy to know that the pilots and the airlines are, in their own interest, making it easier for the pilot to do the right thing rather than the wrong thing should one such exceptional event happen in real life.

Anesthesiologists are now training with computerized mannequins (Gaba, Fish, and Howard 1994) so they will have "done it before" and thus be prepared when some low-occurrence event presents itself in real life. Other medical specialties are also researching the applications of computerized mannequins. Presently such training is conducted for one specialist at a time, although the extension of training to the whole surgery team or to other teams would seem to be straightforward and beneficial.

Nurses and emergency medical personnel use mannequins for cardiopulmonary resuscitation training, water rescue drills, and the like. Mannequins that can generate a range of cardiac patterns on the electrocardiography monitor are used for advanced cardiac life support training. This is all quite positive, and further extension of this training technology would be even better.

Many healthcare organizations carry out disaster drills, which heretofore were commonly designed to consider some industrial disaster appropriate for the area. Currently, disaster drills for terrorist actions are a clear and present need. Companies with offices in the World Trade Center who had taken their fire drills seriously beforehand are now believed to have fared better in the September 11, 2001, tragedy than those who had not; clearly the words of Emerson and the concepts of poka-yoke ring true in this example. Large-scale drills are good both as a means to gaining some practice and as a means to developing workflow data for management to consider.

Repetition

When it comes to error frequency, people follow a bathtub curve. We make mistakes during the early stages as we acquire the skills to do any task. A long flat period follows when mistakes almost never happen. Later, the error rate rises again as people develop bad habits. The flat period can be extended by periodic retraining. For example, airline pilots do periodic simulator retraining even though they fly the same plane every day. Some healthcare certifications require periodic demonstration that the skills are still there; sometimes the same training mannequins are used again. This is good counter-bathtub-curve practice. Consideration should be given to extending this to other skills, both those that are used infrequently and those that are used frequently. Again, another demonstration of poka-yoke.

Healthcare practitioners, as a rule, do many tasks—even complicated ones—from memory rather than following a checklist. Airline pilots follow a checklist every time they take the plane off the ground, even if they take off and land six times a day. Which of these professionals is less likely to skip a step or do things out of sequence? Which is better protected from the bathtub curve? Which practice is in adherence of poka-yoke?

Keying and Interlocks

We use "keying" in the sense of a key used to solve a puzzle. Color, size, shape, weight, and feel are keys that contribute to a person making the right selection and recognizing quickly if he or she has made the wrong selection. Keying shows good poka-yoke.

Interlocks take the decision out of the person's hands and may or may not be a good idea. The earlier example of childproof caps describes an interlock. Five-drawer file cabinets are another type of interlock. They are commonly designed so that only one drawer can be open at a time; this is done for the good reason that the cabinet is apt to fall over on the person pulling on the drawers if the top two drawers are open at the same time. Airlocks between public rooms and controlled-atmosphere rooms are interlocks. Interlocks such as these that deal with only one function are generally good ideas.

The question becomes much more difficult if multiple functions are involved. For example, fire hydrants have large bolt-heads that are to be turned to permit the water to flow, and the bolt-heads have five sides rather than the customary six. This has been done so that a standard wrench will not fit and only the five-sided wrench carried by firemen on the truck will. This is another example of an interlock, and in this case it is used to prevent children from playing with the fire hydrant. But what happens if a legitimate need for water arises and no fire truck is on hand? A day may come when more fires occur than trucks are available to fight them; a bucket brigade will do what it can but is unable to because the hydrant cannot be turned on.

Kitting

Preparing burn kits, gallbladder kits, appendectomy kits, and others is poka-yoke because it makes it easy to have the right set of supplies on hand when a specific treatment is to be performed. The kitting can be done at a time of less stress or even by suppliers. If the kitting is done in-house, providing a key such as a yellow tag when the kit is incomplete is important. Shelf-life needs to be evident. Kitting can be extended to all kinds of services, even to the preparation of insurance forms.

Kits are inventory. Some judgment is required when deciding what kits to make up and which ones are not necessary. If the organization sees one case of lion fever every 20 years, a lion fever kit would not seem to be a good use of working capital.

Computer Displays

Computer displays can generate information overload. The trend—and it is a good one—is to simplify computer displays, to use more diagrammatic presentations, to prioritize alarms, and to make the information understandable to the nonspecialist.

Specialists who understand the complex displays will generally say that the displays are just fine the way they are. The complex displays allow the specialists to apply their mastery and preserve the special knowledge they have acquired. The experts do not see a need for any help, and they do not want any help.

In fields other than healthcare, giving the experts help, even if they do not want it, is found to reduce error rates. You have seen the ground control room NASA uses at Johnson Space Center for space shuttle launches and now for Space Station Freedom. It is a big room with lots of desks, computer displays, and telephones, and it is filled with experts doing important, life-critical tasks. NASA has been operating such rooms for more than 30 years and has learned something about computer-expert interfaces. As computers have become more powerful over the years, NASA has upgraded the computer displays, adding more information but also reorganizing and prioritizing the information so that less-expert humans can understand what is going on. Because of this, NASA has found that the error rate—of errors made by experts—has gone down, and turnover has gone up. These positions, which now require less expertise, are less attractive to the engineering staff. The important thing, though, is that the error rate has gone down.

Perhaps this is the case in the healthcare field, too: even though experts do not want the help, maybe they could use a little anyway, for the good of the cause. Computer displays should make doing the right thing easier than doing the wrong thing by organizing the pertinent information and guiding the person to do the right thing. They should make it obvious, immediately, when the wrong thing has been done. Computer displays should allow a person a second chance by allowing him or her to recover from an error before irreversible action is taken. All of these ideas are not only common sense, they are poka-yoke.

System Reliability

High system reliability can be achieved by providing two or three systems in parallel or as backups. Three systems with 99.9, 99.9, and 99.0 percent reliability rates combine to attain "eight-nines reliability"; just add the nines of the individual systems. This works as long as they have no common modes of failure. A system with eight-nines reliability is expected to be out of service less than one second per year.

Fatigue

Tired people make mistakes. Physical and mental conditioning can help, but the body eventually runs out of gas. In emergencies, fatigue is unavoidable. In everyday operations, on the other hand, fatigue should be avoided by suitable policies. Requiring nurses to work double shifts is inviting mistakes; having staff on call for extended periods is inviting mistakes. Airline pilots may work long flights, but once they are on the ground, they are required by law to stay on the ground until they have had a full eight hours at their hotel.

Essential Equipment

Essential equipment should have sufficient backups on hot standby or cold standby with the backup equipment checked out and ready to go in the same manner as the primary equipment. The reliability of the combined systems should be at least 99.999,999 percent.

The equipment should display its status and let the user know what is going on inside. Modern computerized devices act more and more like black boxes, keeping their doings quite secret. Good design shows a running report or display of what the device is doing at every moment so that the user will know the machine is working and doing things that seem to be reasonable.

Status of Work

The status of all work needs to be evident so that, if some mistake is made, that mistake is evident. For example, putting an x-ray into the viewer in a reversed position is an easy mistake to make. No keying can prevent this error, and the occurrence of this error is not obvious to the technician. This goes against the poka-yoke guidelines. Why are x-ray films not stamped "FRONT" and "BACK" in large letters, or perhaps "RECTO" and "VERSO"? How about a color key?

Patient Location

A particular status issue is the location of each patient. Is the patient in bed? Did the patient get out of bed? The second poka-yoke guideline says that mistakes should be evident so that they can be corrected. If the patient got out of bed on his or her own contrary to instructions, how is the care staff going to know? If the patient decides to leave the care unit on his or her own, how is the care staff going to know? Is every baby in the nursery where it is supposed to be?

Patient Identification

Patient identification bracelets are helpful, but they are not quite perfect. Biometric devices such as retina and face scanners may provide more direct identification in the near future. These scanners require no contact with the person, which would be an advantage over fingerprint scanners. Until some such absolute identification system is practicable, satisfying the poka-yoke guideline to recognize errors immediately will be difficult if the error is in identification. Until such biometric devices are available, what special steps should be taken to reconfirm patient identification prior to any irreversible action?

Pause

Ideally, the worker should be able to pause at any time to take stock for a few moments. Did I do everything? Does this look right? Feel right? Sound right? Is everything on hand for the next step? This ideal may seem like too much to ask, but it is generally possible to design the work plan to build in a pause before each irreversible step.

Allowing for a pause implies no synchronous operations. If Worker A has to keep up with Worker B or Machine C, then Worker A does not have a meaningful opportunity to inject a pause. Because of this, synchronous operations should be avoided. However, this does not exclude parallel operations. Keep in mind that each parallel operation should have points that allow for pause so that other operations can catch up.

Recovery

It would be great if a person could identify an error and recover from it with no harm or risk to the patient or other damage done. This is possible if the number of irreversible steps is few and things are checked carefully before each of those irreversible steps. Again, the concepts of poka-yoke should always be kept in mind.

Stopping the Line

It took more than 50 years, but manufacturers eventually came to understand that every worker, even the one who seems least important, needs to be able to stop the assembly line if something is amiss; it is better to stop the line occasionally for a false alarm than to continue with errors. Because of this belief, stop buttons are now placed all over factories. Claxons sound, and much attention is rendered. Decisions are made, corrections are made if necessary, and then the line starts up again.

Healthcare does not often run on an assembly line, but the message is the same. Consideration should be given to empowering *all* employees to raise questions, point out unusual conditions, and get respectful attention. In high-stress situations, interjections are not automatically welcomed, which is why it took so long to get to this level of understanding even in the "low-stress" factory. This ideal working environment takes time and effort to achieve. It is a good idea, though, and it is poka-yoke, because the even the most insignificant-seeming worker is acting on a perceived error in an effort to prevent it from continuing to happen.

Accounting

Accounting errors are just as aggravating as treatment errors. A particular feature of accounting errors is that they are commonly made by people who do not know they are making an error and consequently cannot remedy the error on the spot. In many cases the data input to the accounting program is not done by the person who has performed the work but rather by someone else working with secondhand or thirdhand information.

Newer systems that use barcode readers in the patient care unit, in the laboratory, in the pharmacy, and in other places avoid this particular weakness of traditional accounting systems. However, the newer systems do not usually reach poka-yoke goals, because no feedback is given to the person operating the barcode reader. A beep may well sound to indicate that the barcode was digested, but there is rarely a report back to that person to show what the effect on the accounting statement turned out to be. This invites the possibility of doubled entries that are not likely to be spotted until the patient does the spotting.

Good poka-yoke practice is to use live data entry by the worker and to feed the accounting result back immediately to the person who is doing the work. That way, the person who actually knows something about the situation can look to see if the accounting entry is right and, if it is not, recognize the error on the spot so that some corrective action can be taken while the event is still fresh in the mind.

Case Administration

Each patient's case involves treatment coding, releases, and other administrative actions, nearly all of which are done by people who are not standing next to the patient. This means that errors can be made that are not immediately obvious; thus application of the poka-yoke guidelines is difficult.

Untimely administrative actions are also errors because they may delay the treatment or discharge of a patient. Creating an administrative system that encourages timely administrative actions is particularly difficult, in healthcare or in any other kind of organization. Management is left with the responsibility for creating an administrative system with a sufficient number of checks built in but without the benefit of feedback that occurs naturally in the caregiving parts of the organization. The combined system should be built on the poka-yoke guidelines: right decisions should be easier to make than wrong ones, errors should be immediately obvious, and correction should be possible on the spot. Timeliness should also be considered. How can the system be designed so that decisions are made as soon as they are ripe rather than some time later? Are the right incentives in place? Is the right information flow happening? Do the decision makers and the decision bases come together at the right time? Are there policy impediments? Do the decision makers even know when the decision is ripe? If they make the wrong decision, how and when do they find out about it? How do they correct errors on the spot?

Buildings and Infrastructure

Fire zones, quarantine zones, isolation zones, and the like all need to be tested. Personnel access to restricted zones needs to be challenged by such means as having tame outsiders try to penetrate the zones. Tame intruders are a better test of a system than any number of paper studies.

Electric backup systems must be ready to go. Diesel generators need to be started periodically and run under load. The reliability of the combined system should be not less than 99.999,999 percent.

Communications systems these days include wireline telephones, wireless radios, and computer networks. Although the combined reliability of these systems can be expected to be quite high (often better than 99.999,999 percent), communications systems are prone to hidden common modes of failure. Building telephone connections to two separate central offices is good practice, but make sure the two connections are not hung on the same poles or run through the same trenches. Wireless telephone calls might be routed through the same central office as the wireline phones, the data network might run through the same central office or use the same poles or trenches, and even radio traffic might be going through the same central offices; the only way to find out is to have the several communications contractors walk their lines and report back to you.

Data networks are subject to attack by pranksters and villains. This is a matter for data network specialists, and it needs to be taken seriously. Having tame outsiders "attack" the data network can be most illuminating. Because the attack techniques seem to be evolving continually, this is an abiding concern that will be with us until somebody figures out how to make a secure data network. The same applies for water supplies, drains, special gases, and other systems important to patient care. The status of the essential building services should be displayed at all times not only for the plant engineer but for senior management as well.

Poka-yoke comes into play in these infrastructure systems in their design and operation. First, the fundamental design needs to be free from hidden error, and the operating panels and control stations need to be designed so that doing the right thing is always easier than doing the wrong thing. Second, the poka-yoke guidelines say that errors—or in this case, off-normal conditions—need to be evident so they can be redressed. Third, the design of the systems needs to be such that the operator can easily recover from any error.

Medication

Medication errors are thought to be among the most common serious errors in healthcare and include errors made in prescription, pharmacy dispensing, handling by staff, and handling by the patient in self-medicating circumstances (Joint Commission 1998).

The first poka-yoke guideline obviously applies to getting the right prescription rather than the wrong one. The second and third poka-yoke guidelines apply not only to the physician but to everybody else in the chain. How can the pharmacist spot a possible error? How can the staff nurse spot an error at the patient's bedside? How can the patient, sent home with a list of medications, spot an error? If the patient does something wrong at home, how does that patient recognize the error and know what remedial action to take?

Computerized physician's orders, computerized crosschecking by the pharmacist, and barcode tracking of medication and patient all go in the right direction, but they focus only on the first guideline and do not do much in the way of making evident those few errors that creep through the checks, and they do nothing to facilitate recovery actions. For the discharged patient doing self-medication at home, the situation is less structured, and control is lacking. Still, thoughtful application of poka-yoke may provide some help. Predischarge training of the patient and the at-home family care provider can help. Postdischarge retraining by visiting nurses can also help.

This pre- and postdischarge training should cover all of the three poka-yoke guidelines:

1. how to organize the medication and schedule to make taking the right medicine at the right time easier than taking the wrong medicine or taking it at the wrong time;
2. how to recognize an error on the spot; and
3. what to do when an error is made.

Covering the first of these guidelines when designing training plans is natural. However, covering the second and third will take some conscious thought because it may be construed as detracting from the primary message, which is, "Do this the way I am telling you to do it." Still, people make mistakes, and the second and third guidelines need to be part of the patient training package.

The Tell-Tale

Some actions have no obvious effect, so the second poka-yoke guideline cannot be applied. In these cases, the person cannot immediately tell if the action was done correctly or if it was even done at all. In addition, it is not obvious how any supervisor can verify that the action was taken in such situations. For instance, certain patients are supposed to be moved about in their wheelchairs every two hours to prevent pressure ulcers; however, it is hard to know whether this action has taken place every time.

Adding a tell-tale might help. A tell-tale is any feature that tells the tale, such as a little flag on the wheelchair, red on one side and yellow on the other, that is reversed each time the patient's position is adjusted. Before-and-after photographs would work, too, and they would create a permanent record. Clipboard checkoff goes in the same direction, although this method tends to get less diligent attention than others might. Other situations that are difficult to observe also pose challenges. Did Mrs. Jones take her after-dinner pills, or did she slip them in among the remnants on the tray?

Employee Security

The rate of assaults on healthcare workers is five times as high as that on workers in general, and injuries and deaths do occur (Gribbin 2002).

An injury to an employee is of the same gravity as injury to a patient, and steps need to be taken.

Poka-yoke can perhaps be of some assistance in the design of policies to increase the likelihood of making the right decision when identifying threats posed by patients and others and taking preventive measures such as restraints and physical barriers when the risk is nonnegligible.

Many questions must be considered. How can the person who poses a threat of assault be identified? Must there be a prior record? Physical indicators? Warnings received? How is an error in identification recognized as quickly as possible? Have menacing actions or threats been made? How can an error in identification be recovered from before damage is done? Are escape routes or guards nearby?

This is a troubling subject, and the needs of organizations vary widely. Perhaps the poka-yoke discipline can be of some assistance.

WORKFLOW

The measure of success is the rate at which treatments are successfully completed; what counts is the rate at which work flows through the organization. One item of work is the patient, and getting the patient to "flow" through the treatment facility in the minimum amount of time is the best use of the facility. Poor workflow leads to higher census and higher treatment cost for the same number of successful treatments.

The organization and the facility have all kinds of constraints on capacity, and those constraints need to be understood so that the workflow can be managed in the best way. Any facility or service process has two kinds of operations: bottlenecks and non-bottlenecks. Recognizing which ones are which is the first step toward improving workflow.

The Bottleneck

Consider the office of a family dentist, a sole practitioner with an established practice. Let us take a look at the workflow in the dentist's office. First of all, there is a bottleneck, which can be identified as the dentist herself. Suppose our dentist takes 20 minutes off in the middle of the afternoon; that represents 20 minutes of time with no production. Will patients wait an extra 20 minutes so that our dentist can make up the lost production by extending her workday 20 minutes? Maybe, but a patient might walk out, and more than one patient might start shopping for a more committed dentist. Can the dentist make up for the lost production by working faster on the next three patients? Maybe, but hurrying might trigger an error that would then take even more time to correct, thereby delaying production all the more and putting the patient in question on the list of those shopping for a new dentist. In short, any productive time lost at the bottleneck is production lost forever.

Furthermore, any productive time lost for any reason at all is production lost forever. If the patient is late, if the patient's records are not in order, if the dentist's drills are not cleaned and ready, if the novocaine supply runs out, if the hand tools are not out of the sterilizer, if the bib supply runs out, if any of a million little things goes wrong, productive time is lost forever. Knowing this, the dentist makes an effort to make sure that everything is ready and to double-check her system before each patient is put in the chair. Meanwhile, pains are taken to make sure the patient arrives and that payment is assured by checking the insurance authorization before the patient gets in the chair.

So, with the patient present and qualified and with the system double-checked, the bottleneck work gets underway. This is the most productive the dentist can make her office. The dentist also makes sure that as little dead-time as possible transpires between patients. Cleaning up after one patient and getting ready for the next is nonproductive time. Our dentist may invest in a second room and chair so that the setup time for each successive patient is near zero; this maximizes productive time at the bottleneck.

Suppose the dentist's son graduates from dental school and joins the practice. Suddenly there is a twofold expansion of the bottleneck; suddenly there is spare capacity; suddenly the practice is scrambling to expand the clientele population and thinking up new services to offer to soak up that excess capacity. Over time this growth in clientele should fill up the new, expanded bottleneck.

Let us suppose, however, that no way is found to get the clientele population up to twice the former level. What should the dentists do? They should reduce capacity because having idle capacity is pointless. The dentist's son might go back to school part-time to study laser bonding to expand the service offerings. The dentist herself might take one day off a week to contribute her time to a charity clinic or to write the definitive book on dental practice.

Our dentists probably considered the market pretty carefully before they decided to double the capacity of their little organization, so they were likely able to fill the new capacity pretty quickly. Their business is simple to analyze, and because they run it directly themselves, they surely thought things through before making the change.

Upstream

You know how dentists deal with things upstream of the bottleneck (the bottleneck being themselves). Patients are booked to arrive several minutes before the dentist actually plans to see them so that any minor lateness on the part of the patient does not trigger a loss of production in the bottleneck. The reception clerk checks records and insurance formalities before the patient gets called to the chair.

Suppose the standard dental treatment time is 20 minutes and the standard reception processing time is 5 minutes. The reception clerk can process four patients in the time it takes the dentist to do one. Should the reception clerk then work ahead, processing as many patients as he or she can to be as productive as possible? No! The reception clerk should be *idle* 15 minutes out of every 20. Getting extra patients in and processed only means that patients will be waiting longer to see the dentist, fuming all the while and contemplating what to tell the neighbors about the high-handedness of this dentist. Keeping the reception clerk busy is not a goal of the organization.

The reception clerk may be given other, low-priority duties to soak up idle time, but the standing orders to the reception clerk are to have the next patient processed before the dentist is ready for that patient and with a few minutes' slack. Attention is paid to the bottleneck because the bottleneck is the limit on production.

Downstream

The discharge clerk should process the outgoing patient promptly, so that outgoing patients do not get stacked up at the discharge desk and, sympathetically, so that the patients do not contemplate shopping for a different dentist.

Suppose the standard discharge-processing time is 5 minutes, and suppose our dentists' treatment time is again 20 minutes. The discharge clerk should also be idle 15 minutes out of every 20. The discharge clerk should certainly not make patients sit around and wait until a sufficient batch of them is available to make the discharge clerk's work as productive as possible.

The discharge clerk may be given other, low-priority duties, such as making sure the magazines on the rack are sufficiently out of date so that patients are not tempted to sit down in the waiting room to finish that article, thereby clogging up the space. The standing orders to the discharge clerk are always to get that outgoing patient moved promptly, dropping other work to attend to the outgoing patient. Attention is paid to the bottleneck because the bottleneck is the limit on production. The productivity of the discharge clerk is not important.

Kanban

Dentists always knew what Japanese factory managers discovered for themselves and called kanban. Kanban is the Anglicized version of the Japanese word for punched-card. The work-authorization form was a punch-card, and the name for the card came to be the name for the production strategy. The Japanese decided that the right way to run a factory is to keep the work flowing continuously through the factory bottleneck and to keep workers upstream of the bottleneck idle until authorized to produce work to flow into the bottleneck. It works for factories just as it works for dentists' offices.

Goldratt and Cox (1984) has elaborated this into a general theory of production. The essence of the Goldratt theory is as follows:

1. The production of the bottleneck is the production of the organization.
2. Production upstream of the bottleneck should be on-demand and idle until demand arises.
3. Production downstream of the bottleneck should be idle until work comes to it from the bottleneck.

Is this not a simple theory? Does not every dentist already know this? Yet it is profound. Every organization has a bottleneck. Every organization has activities upstream of the bottleneck. Every organization has activities downstream of the bottleneck. To be specific, every healthcare service has a bottleneck, activities upstream of the bottleneck, and activities downstream of the bottleneck. Recognizing this truism is important because the management interest in each of the three phases is distinct.

Why Is There a Bottleneck?

A bottleneck exists because the cost of expanding the bottleneck is so great as to be prohibitive. In financial terms, the cost to expand the bottleneck is so great that a negative financial impact continues throughout the financial planning period. This cost might be the cost of the extra dentist in our case above, the cost of building an expansion of the pediatric care unit, or the cost of another magnetic resonance imaging machine. It might be the shortage of skilled personnel such as heart surgeons or specialized nurses.

In healthcare, bottlenecks may be created by regulation, such as a limit on the number of beds set by a regional commission. Bottlenecks may be imposed by the size of the physical facilities. There is always a bottleneck.

What happens if so many dentists offer services in a town that there are not enough patients to go around and no prospect of much growth in demand? Is that not the absence of a bottleneck? Yes, and the right response is to reduce capacity until a bottleneck occurs again. Drive the weakest practices out, buy up some others, and get the capacity down. If this does not happen, the aggregate economics are ruinous. In businesses with any prospect of survival, there is always a bottleneck.

Management at the Bottleneck

Because any delay that affects the bottleneck affects the organization as a whole in direct measure, the operational focus is on making sure the bottleneck equipment is in order, all supplies are on hand, the staff are trained up to high standards, the patient is double-checked, and all patient records are double-checked. Any lost production at the bottleneck cannot be recovered, so the focus has to be on making sure that no production is lost at the bottleneck.

Any setup time in the bottleneck, even such mundane things as making up a bed, requires management attention to make sure that it is done correctly and promptly, because setup time is a direct detractor to the capacity of the bottleneck and therefore a direct detractor to the capacity of the entire system.

Bottlenecks

- Every service has a true bottleneck resulting from physical capacity limits or regulations.
- If work is piling up elsewhere, it is because of an error in workflow management.
- Do not overcommit the bottleneck; save something as surge capacity.
- Do not worry about capacity in non-bottleneck locations because these locations can always catch up.

Both work and management at the bottleneck are intense. On the other hand, the bottleneck is easy to manage because the employees can see exactly how important their work is, there is plenty of work to do, and management gives plenty of attention. Budgets for upkeep and upgrade are easily justified.

Management Upstream of the Bottleneck

The focus upstream of the bottleneck is on making sure that the patient is ready to go to the bottleneck when the bottleneck is ready for the patient. Working ahead is not productive and is likely to annoy the patient by creating long waits in queue.

Workers upstream are idle much of the time. They need to be idle so that they can jump into action when triggered by notice from the bottleneck.

Having idle workers is anathema to the cost accounting department. Workers themselves do not like to be idle, especially skilled workers. And yet that is the optimum production strategy: capacity on-call (or, to say it another way, idleness until called) upstream of the bottleneck. This practice is accepted for firefighters (one wonders how cost accounting works for a fire brigade . . .). It should also be accepted for any activity that jumps into action when the call comes.

While upstream of the bottleneck, firefighters play checkers and wash the truck. Upstream healthcare workers can take up lower-priority work when idle from their main duties, or they can even play checkers, as long as they stay at the ready for their principal duties when the call comes. Although the patient is the most important workflow item, the same logic applies to any department that feeds into the bottleneck department, including supplies, pharmacy, records, accounts, and so on.

Investments to increase capacity upstream are suspect given that excess capacity already exists. Projects that would reduce capacity upstream are possible if capital assets are freed up and the projects are designed so that a new bottleneck not be created.

Management Downstream of the Bottleneck

Downstream of the bottleneck, there is nothing to do until the work presents itself. Downstream there is excess capacity, so any minor loss of production is not a loss of production by the organization. A complete breakdown downstream will eventually stall the bottleneck and become a limit on the production of the organization.

Workers and equipment will be idle between episodes of work. Workers can be given low-priority work to fill the idle minutes, but the standing order has to be to jump-to when the work arrives. This is easy to manage, although most professional employees do not welcome idleness.

Investments to increase capacity downstream are suspect given that excess capacity already exists. Projects that would reduce capacity downstream are possible if capital assets are freed up and the projects are designed so that a new bottleneck is not created.

Bottleneck Placement

By and large, the nature of each organization dictates where the bottleneck will be. The extent to which management can control the placement of the bottleneck may indicate how easy it can see where the best place would be. The best place for the bottleneck is *not* at the end of the process. Everyone who shops at a grocery store is infuriated by the grocery store bottleneck: the checkout counters.

The right place to have a bottleneck is at the first step in the process. Some big-name theme parks throttle the number of patrons allowed into the park so that the patrons will not have to wait interminably in queue to ride the popular rides. They put the bottleneck at the first step of their service process; that is the best place to have it.

Even though the ideal place for the bottleneck is recognized, most organizations find that their bottleneck is in the middle just by the nature of the business, and management can do nothing about it. The ideal is not attainable.

Managing the Workflow

Three management regimes apply to the three segments of the workflow (bottleneck, upstream, and downstream). Because the production of the organization rests on the production of the bottleneck, workflow management starts from the bottleneck and works in both directions.

1. Identify the bottleneck. Apply maximum-net-production management rules to the bottleneck activity. Work to reduce nonproductive

bottleneck time such as machine setup time or room changeover time. Have workers on the bench to pinch hit for absent productive personnel. Work on preventive maintenance, skill training, and retention. Analyze every detail, and look to improve yield. Apply poka-yoke to every task because any error in the bottleneck will take time to fix and will reduce productive capacity.

2. Identify upstream work. Apply idle-until-called-on management rules for upstream activity. Reduce variability to reduce risk in being late to the bottleneck. Think poka-yoke. Check thoroughly for errors and correct them on the spot because errors propagating into the bottleneck are not desired.

3. Identify downstream work. Apply idle-until-work-arrives management rules for downstream activity. Reduce variability to reduce risk of backing workflow up into the bottleneck. Think poka-yoke. Check thoroughly for errors and correct them on the spot.

The negative expressions of those same rules are these:

1. Do not lose production at the bottleneck for want of preparation or for want of double-checking the equipment, the staff, and the patient prior to doing the bottleneck work. Do not make mistakes in the bottleneck that will require rework in the bottleneck and a loss of production.

2. Do not confuse busyness with production upstream, thereby risking a loss of work for the bottleneck by failing to have the upstream staff or facilities ready to respond to the call. Do not make mistakes upstream that will propagate into the bottleneck.

3. Do not confuse busyness with production downstream, which may cause queuing up of patients even to the extent of backing up into the bottleneck. Do not make mistakes downstream that will back work up into the bottleneck or send rework back to the bottleneck.

Surge Capacity

Honda is a well-managed Japanese car manufacturer. The Honda practice is to commit no more than 80 percent of a factory's capacity so that, if something goes wrong at the factory bottleneck, surge capacity is available to catch up to commitments. The financial argument against this policy is obvious because it means that 20 percent of the factory's capacity is not used most of the time with a concomitant low return on assets.

This is an interesting balancing of interests. To keep customers happy, hold back some surge capacity so that the organization can catch up quickly to commitments. To keep accountants happy, hold nothing back. Honda thinks customers are more important than accountants. What do you think? Twenty percent may be too much surge capacity for most organizations, but zero is probably too little. Management should consider the Honda management model and make a conscious policy decision. Dentists might make a practice of not booking a half-hour in the middle of the afternoon to provide for some surge capacity.

The Kinds of Waits

Workflow involves the transfer of patients or material from one work center to another. In healthcare, this is unlikely to be done by assembly line, so the workflow rate is not going to be uniform. Because the flow is not uniform, some time will be spent waiting. It is instructive to consider the different types of waiting that apply.

Removing all waits is not possible, but knowing what types of waits exist, which ones are there on purpose, and which ones are not is a good idea. Waiting consumes resources because waiting extends the treatment time.

Queuing

Queuing is waiting for service. Queuing is appropriate and even necessary at the bottleneck because it is important to the organization that the bottleneck never run out of work.

The length of the queue at the bottleneck can be set in a design rule such as, "a queue of sufficient length such that the likelihood that the bottleneck will run out of work is less than one percent on any day."

This turns on two things: the predictability of the workload in the bottleneck and the predictability of the time required to move the next patient to the bottleneck. Both are amenable to study and quantification.

Pending

Pending is waiting for administrative release. Because this is not exactly the same as waiting for physical work to be completed, pending waits are largely under administrative control.

Consider the administrative step of getting the admitting physician to discharge a patient. Some physical or mental work is required of the physician to review the case and sign the release. The administrative part is finding the physician, presenting the file, and waiting for the discharge order to be signed. This can be improved by providing roller skates to the file messenger, electronic mail to the physician, or other suitable means.

Other administrative tasks may be pending, such as social service reports, family authorizations, rehabilitation facility acceptance, credit approvals, and so on. Each needs to be addressed in a distinct way because any improvement will not likely apply across the board when dealing with such a varied population.

Batching

Batching is the intentional grouping of patients or other work so that one setup can be used several times. Batching the work of the bottleneck is appropriate if some setup time is required at the bottleneck because that setup time is nonproductive. Using the same setup several times in a row by batching the work minimizes the nonproductive portion of the day and maximizes production

An inviting target for improvement at the bottleneck is to reduce setup time by bringing in new technology or perhaps by reorganizing the work. Reducing bottleneck setup time is good on its own because it reduces nonproductive time at the bottleneck.

Batching increases variability in the overall service performance time. Patients at the head of the batch are processed in less overall time than patients at the end of a batch; smaller batches are thus an indicator of improving overall system time.

Batching anywhere upstream or downstream is suspect. Because excess capacity exists everywhere other than at the bottleneck, reducing non-bottleneck setup time is not an obvious goal. Since batching increases overall service time variability, batching is probably a negative except when it occurs at the bottleneck.

Bunching

Bunching is the unintentional grouping of patients or other work. Bunching is usually caused by others. Bunching is a surge of service demand or a surge of workflow into an activity. Dealing with that surge in demand requires resources.

Orthodontists serving the teenage market for braces face the fact that their demand will surge after school hours, and they figure that into their organization resource planning. British emergency rooms can figure on a bunch of bleeding fans after major soccer matches.

Within the healthcare organization, bunching is an artifact of local optimization. For example, if the surgery department keeps all patients until the end of the shift and then sends them all to the postoperative patient care unit in a bunch, that may (or may not) be optimum for the surgery department, but it certainly presents the postoperative patient care unit with a surge of patients to handle. This may be the optimum policy for the organization, but it is suspect.

The pharmacy may deliver all medicine orders to a patient care unit in bunches, one or two times per shift, to reduce the cost of messengers and carts. This may be the right policy because it allows the patient care unit manager to focus on medicine at those few times per shift, and it probably does not change the overall medicine inventory level very much for the organization. The same is true for ordinary supply deliveries.

Bunching tends to increase the variability of overall service time and is therefore generally suspect. It tends to require surge capacity, and it is suspect for that reason as well.

Hanging

Hanging, or hanging up, is waiting while some parallel process is completed. This may be as simple a matter as waiting for the delivery of routine supplies or waiting for an essential person required for the next task.

FIGURE 3: TIME-VALUE CHART FOR X-RAY VISIT

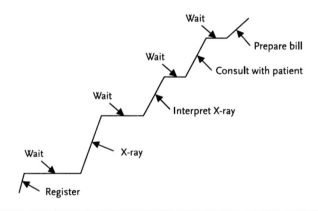

Time-Value Charts

Consider the case of the patient who comes to a health service center for a diagnostic x-ray and advice from her doctor. Let us look at the time line to see where value is being added and where no value is being added.

In the chart on the opposite page, time proceeds to the right, and added value causes the chart to grow upward. At the first step, the patient registers and presents personal information, which is a necessary part of the service and so adds value. Following that step is a wait, during which no value is added. The x-ray is then taken, which adds value. Then another wait occurs, which adds no value. The x-ray is interpreted by the doctor or doctors, and this adds value. A wait follows, which adds no value. A consultation is made with the patient, which adds value. Then another wait occurs, which adds no value. The bill is prepared, and this adds value. The patient then leaves, thereby completing the exercise.

Note that the meaning of "value" here indicates an activity's value to the organization. The patient might be tempted to think that preparing the bill is not adding value (to his or her side of things), but of course it is from the organization's point of view. Note further that the value is being added by a variety of actors including the patient, the admitting clerk, the x-ray technician, the medical doctors, the invoicing clerk, and perhaps others.

The vertical rise associated with each value-adding step is loosely proportional to the incremental value, but no particular precision is required. This is a sketch, not an accounting statement. The time lapses, on the other hand, should be tracked with some care, because it is time that draws our attention here. The utility of a time-value chart is that it makes obvious where the time lapses with no value are occurring. Getting rid of some of the gaps speeds up the overall service while detracting not at all from the value added.

A time-value chart is simple, yet it portrays much about the workings of the system. Why is each particular wait there? Why does it last as long as it does? What would be the benefit, if any, of reducing the wait? What is the cost to the organization of that wait? What is the cost to the patient, in lost time, for that wait?

The rules that govern workflow are necessarily management rules. Furthermore, they must be set at a senior management level to preclude one department from solving its problems by moving them to the next department. The senior management can issue rational workflow rules only if it understands where the bottleneck is, why it is there, and what the incentives are to keep the bottleneck flowing. Hence, the senior management can develop and issue rules that govern flow through the bottleneck and through the upstream and downstream departments.

Senior management will also gain a basis for evaluating capital requests for the expansion of various departments. Will that capital expansion expand the bottleneck? If not, why is it being considered? Perhaps certain departments should be contracted to free up resources that would expand the bottleneck.

Batch of One

From the point of view of the patient, the right batch size is one: the individual patient. In the patient's perfect scenario, there would be no waiting in queue at the magnetic resonance imaging machine, no waiting for pending administrative actions, and no bunching up with other patients to suit the convenience of one service or another. This scenario would automatically be the case if it were also the least-cost way of doing things for the healthcare organization. It is not yet so, but the trend is in that direction.

As more and more healthcare functions are computerized, mechanized, and even robotized, the incentive to batch patients goes down because, as the setup cost goes to zero, the most productive batch size goes to one.

In non-bottleneck departments, the size of batch is arbitrary because plenty of slack is inherent by definition. In these departments, much could be done today to move in the direction of batch-of-one patient management.

At the bottleneck, where setup time needs to be shared over a batch of patients because it is a dead loss to the whole organization, capital investments to reduce setup time provide a twofold benefit. First, the productive capacity of the whole organization goes up. A second advantage is that the optimum batch size goes toward one, which pleases patients.

Problem Solving

Problems are solved by examining events, figuring out what went wrong, and deciding what might work better. Six Sigma provides a systematic management method to respond to events both to make sure that the event does not repeat itself and to be confident that long-term remedies are evaluated prudently before being applied to the whole of the organization.

EVENTS

Causality

Chicago, October 8, 1871. Mrs. O'Leary's cow accidentally kicks over a kerosene lantern and sets fire to straw on the barn floor. The fire spreads, leaving 80,000 people homeless and 300,000 without drinking water. Twenty-six hundred acres of residential, commercial, and industrial real estate went up in smoke (*Chicago Tribune* 1871). What caused this fire? The lantern? The dry straw? The dry weather? The cow? Historians have long since exonerated Mrs. O'Leary, but the official cause remains up to debate.

Aristotle said that every event has three causes: a material cause, a proximate cause, and an efficient cause. The efficient cause is the person who took the action that triggered the proximate cause, which in turn activated the material cause, all of which together caused the event to happen.

In Chicago on that fateful day, Mrs. O'Leary's abundant flammables were the material cause, the lantern was the proximate cause, and Mrs. O'Leary's cow was the efficient cause.

Aristotle Said
Events Have
Three Causes

1. Material
   Cause
2. Proximate
   Cause
3. Efficient
   Cause

Therefore, every
party can shift the
blame onto two
others, with some
justification.

When looking at events, it is useful to start with Aristotle and sort out the material, proximate, and efficient causes if only to have an immediate appreciation that every party involved will have two others to point at, each with some logic on his or her side. Without the other two causes, the event would not have happened at that time and place. It might have happened at another time and place, but if the focus is on exactly one event, every interested party can point at two others. The "flammables guy" can point at the lantern and the cow, the "lantern guy" can point at the flammables and at the cow, and the cow . . . well, the cow cannot very well point and will probably wind up with the blame.

Chain of Events

Why was that lantern placed where the cow could knock it over? Who put the lantern there? Why was that person in the barn after dark? Why was a kerosene lantern being used instead of a safety lamp of some kind (remembering that this was 1871 and technology was somewhat quaint)? Why was the cow there, in the middle of Chicago? Who was in charge of the cow? Was the cow sufficiently constrained so as to preclude kicking over lanterns? Why was all that straw there? Why was it not wetted down to preclude ignition? Where was the nearest fire extinguisher? Who called the fire brigade? Where was the nearest fire station?

Walking through the chain of events is informative. Keeping in mind that three causes occur in chains of events is helpful, and trying to deal with everything in one chain often causes a jumble. Management needs to trace through the chains of events and take steps immediately to break those chains—or to break one of them at the very least—so that the same unhappy thing cannot happen again immediately. Not doing so would not be prudent management.

Yet this is not sufficient. The exact same chain of events will not likely happen again, but something similar may well happen, and it is important that steps be taken to anticipate such problems and find a more general solution.

The Three-Plane Model

Some industries study events by considering them on three planes:

1. mechanisms

2. conditions

3. constraints

On the mechanism plane go the chains of events and mechanistic analyses such as failure modes and effects.

FIGURE 4: THE THREE-PLANE MODEL

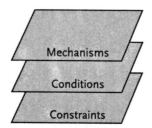

On the conditions plane go the circumstances that applied to the development of the situation. For the Chicago fire, the circumstances were hot, dry, weather; crowded construction; fire brigades sufficient to handle only two local fires a day; no fire-warning telegraph callboxes in residential areas; doubtful construction standards for residential areas; illumination by fire in lanterns and gas lamps; and horses and cows kept in residential areas.

On the constraints plane go the policies, regulations, laws, standards, and other administrative controls that bear on the circumstances. Again, in the case of the Chicago fire, these would include fire codes, zoning, brigade staffing rules, callbox placement, animal control regulations, and fire-watch staffing. The constraints plane is where management can control the conditions that govern the chain of events.

The city managers of Chicago might have considered the conditions and concluded that they could not do much about animal control because horses and cows were needed for transportation and milk production. They could not do much about construction standards because wooden construction was the only thing likely to be practicable in the Midwest. On the other hand, they could do something about construction density, perhaps carving out fire breaks by putting major road arteries every quarter of a mile or so to contain any future fire into one large square. They could add more fire stations. They could add more telegraph fire callboxes. They could require that a bucket of sand be kept in every barn. They could put up warning posters and enact laws against leaving lanterns unattended in barns. They could do several of these things, expecting more results from some than from others.

Sorting information out and putting it on these three conceptual planes (mechanisms, conditions, and constraints) takes time and effort. However, it is usually time and effort well-spent because to gives management a frame of reference to use when considering new policies.

DIGGING IN

An event has happened, and you want to know why. You want to know how to make sure, as best you can, that it does not happen again. It takes digging to find the facts, to find the chains of events, to find the circumstances, and to find the policies, rules, and regulations that were to be followed. Indeed, were they followed? If not, was it for a good reason?

When doing this digging, it is useful to find a comparable event that was "normal" so that distinctions can be found between the normal and the abnormal event. The first scientific principle is that effects flow from prior causes, that a change in outcome must flow from some change in the operation. Perhaps the change is due to normal fluctuations in operations; this matter will be taken up later in this book. At this point, we will attend to events that were sufficiently far out of the ordinary that they were called directly to the attention of management.

The management interest in digging into such events is to find something management can do to control future events. What policies need attention? What technology needs attention? What staffing or training need attention? What capital facilities need attention? What stop-gap measures should be implemented immediately to break the chain of events?

In doing the digging, some diagrammatic tools have been found to be helpful. These will be taken up shortly. Diagrams are helpful because, in most cases, the hard facts are only part of the story. People may well have seen different—even contradictory—things. People with an interest in the case may have different interests to protect or project. Any gaps in the story may be filled in differently by different people. Differences almost always are found between the stated policy on how things are done and how they are actually done, and these differences might be important and might not come to light if the investigation is not thorough.

People are naturally defensive if something untoward has happened on their watch. However, defensive people are not very helpful at producing unbiased information. Getting the cooperation of these people, who are the very ones who probably know the most about what has happened, is pretty important for getting to the bottom of problems.

Proceeding in a nonjudgmental way is important, and that is where diagrams come into play. The diagrams do not make any judgment, and they are one way of getting the cooperation of people who are not inclined to cooperate.

The best way to get such cooperation is to establish a track record of being nonjudgmental, of treating people reasonably, and of not punishing the messenger. That takes time, and it takes a consistent approach across senior management, but it can be done. Indeed, one of the most important contributions executive management can make is to clarify the thinking on this matter for the middle management.

COMPARE AND CONTRAST

Start with the event itself and some comparable case that had the expected outcome. Figure out the chains of events. Get anecdotal input. Use group meetings and diagrams. Look for the input or operation that distinguishes the two cases. There must be at least one difference; several may be evident, but there is at least one.

Compare and Contrast

Study the event, and study a comparable event that had a normal outcome.

In some cases, a benchmark case is available that is thoroughly documented and that can serve as the reference case. When first starting out, benchmark cases may not be at hand, but as you apply the Six Sigma management method over time, benchmark cases will make themselves available naturally.

Dig deeper into each of the differences. Suspend judgment, if humanly possible, until all of the differences are understood. The rule of thumb is to dig until you think you have identified the source of the problem, then dig deeper, and then dig deeper again. Although this can get out of hand, it is good to dig deep enough to be sure that nothing is hidden just below the present level of examination.

Benchmarks Help

As you apply Six Sigma, you will acquire benchmarks that will provide direct bases for comparison.

Categories of Difficulties

We will now take a look at some likely categories of difficulties.

Worker Error

The first thing to do is to change the heading to something other than "Worker Error" because that starts the whole process with a witch-hunt ambiance. We will start again.

Design of Work

Did the event happen because of an error in carrying out a task? How is the work task designed? Does it conform to poka-yoke guidelines? Has the worker been trained and retrained? Does this task get done correctly on the day shift but not on the other shifts? Does this task get done correctly by some groups but not by other groups? What is the training or qualification policy that governs this task? How is the task actually done?

Experienced workers commonly ignore the official directions and do tasks the way they think they should be done. Often, they are right; after all, they do the task all the time, and the efficiency expert who wrote the procedure is long gone. Sometimes, though, they are wrong, and it is necessary to find out what is really being done so the matter can be sorted out.

Equipment Failure

Did the event happen because of equipment failure? Equipment failure may not seem to be a management issue, but it is. Management needs to provide sufficient backup and fail-over equipment so that the combined system, with primary and backup equipment considered, is very robust. Therefore, the management interest is in knowing what backup equipment is on hand, how it is deployed, how people are trained to switch over to backups at the critical moment (which is when primary equipment always fails) without loss of function, and how the primary and backup equipment are maintained and certified for use.

If the backup equipment operates differently, the operators must be qualified to work on both the primary and backup equipment. If knobs are to be turned in the opposite direction on the backup equipment, trouble lurks.

Equipment breakdowns in this age of computer marvels are less frequent than they used to be, and this is a great thing. However, it also means that attention needs to be paid to drilling people in doing the switchover because they may never have done it in their normal course of work.

Hidden Equipment Malfunction

Did the event happen because of a hidden malfunction of the equipment? A serious question in the computer age is whether the equipment is working or not. Although a well-designed machine will provide a running display of what it is doing and keep track of its internal workings itself, with suitable reports to the operator, the machine is probably only checking itself on the inside. The machine probably cannot tell if its hoses are connected correctly or even if they are connected at all. The same is true for electrical leads and other connective devices.

External verification is important. This may be achieved with a separate instrument or by operator observation of signals distinct from those on the machine, such as patient manifestations or other indirect signs.

Although this is a system-level consideration and not a work-task consideration, system design can take advantage of poka-yoke, too. Is it easier for the operator to interpret the indirect signals correctly than not? Are mistakes (in this case, equipment malfunctions) immediately obvious? Does the operator have some means of correcting matters on the spot? Malfunction drills help, particularly drills that involve a whole team of people.

Internal Surge in Demand

Was the event triggered by a surge in demand that for some reason was internal to the organization? Was this because of an emergency? A blunder in scheduling? A policy that helped one department by creating an overload in another? Was there, on the other hand, an unplanned shortfall in capacity because of personnel scheduling, fatigued staff, or an expected demand for personnel elsewhere?

External Surge in Demand

Was the event triggered by a surge in demand that was for some reason external to the organization? If so, the likelihood of something going wrong is increased. Although external events are by definition beyond the control of the organization, the question may be asked if the organization has considered external events in its capacity planning in a reasonable way.

Forest fires occur in California every February. Forest fires usually mean injuries. What planning basis does a healthcare organization use, the 50-year fire, the 100-year fire, the 1-year fire, or the 5-year fire? If the facility is near a freeway where multicar accidents happen, is the organization prepared for the 50-year crash, the 10-year crash, or even the 1-year crash?

The same must be considered for building fires, factory explosions, earthquakes, floods, and other external events that can be predicted to happen at some time but not with any precision in the timing. What service level does management establish for such expected but unpredictable events? Does management have enough information in hand about the consequences of such events that a reasonable policy can be established?

Infrastructure

Did an infrastructure breakdown contribute to the event? Infrastructure is usually a combination of public services and internal backup services. Water is purchased from the local water company, and in addition the facility has its own water tank with, for example, a four-hour inventory to take care of any upsets in the public supply. Is the sizing basis for the internal backup up-to-date? What is the public company's outage experience? Is some policy in place to cut down on water use during the on-internal-tankage period? Does the facility engineer, management, or both know when water is being drawn from the internal tanks?

Public electric supply is subject to outages. Most facilities of any size provide themselves with a local electric diesel generator that starts immediately when the public supply is interrupted. In addition, vital electrical loads have battery backup. Although the details of the diesel loading sequence and the maintenance of each battery system are a matter for the engineering staff, the management issue arises from the growth in electrical demand as more and more computerized devices are added. Is the demand following the established capacity plan? Is attention being paid by the electric company? Is the electric company providing two feeds to the facility so that one knocked-over pole someplace in their territory will not shut down electric service to the facility? Are the diesels up-to-date and ample in capacity? Is a rational sizing rule in place for each battery system? The same types of questions must be considered for communications systems and for any data networking and external computer services.

Services provided by trucks have the same characteristics and hardwired infrastructures. Consider the supplies of medicine, special gases, and other supplies. What is the reliability of the external suppliers and trucking service providers? Is the inventory of each set by some reasonable rule based on robust service rather than on economic order quantities?

Unplanned Circumstances

Was the event caused by circumstances not considered in prior planning? For instance, if the patient care unit has three patients all named John J. Anderson, the normal type of patient nametag may not be of much use in keeping track if the nametag system design does not anticipate duplicate names. This situation would be even more serious if the nursery had three babies named John J. Anderson.

Unplanned Events

Was the event so unusual that it was simply beyond the planning bases that the organization has in place? Some maladies exist that few practitioners have seen, either because they are very near to eradication from the planet or because they only exist in some far-distant land. A traveler on safari in Kenya might acquire lion fever and bring it home, developing symptoms only on his or her return. Would any local doctor recognize lion fever? Is it reasonable that any local doctor should or that the organization be prepared to deal with a lion fever case? Does the organization have a planning basis for responding to new demands for services that might be quite sudden in onset? Elective eye surgery for vision correction is a current example of this situation.

Computer Issues

Did the event involve computer systems? The naïve view of computers is that once the computer program is debugged, it will give the right answer every time. This is no longer true. Computer programs upgrade themselves, unbidden, by connecting to their home web page. Although this is a good way of keeping things up-to-date and while it almost always works, the fact is that you cannot be sure at any moment whether the computer program is running properly. The vendor did not make those last 27 changes with your particular needs in mind. Operating systems, application programs, network operating systems, remote data sources, firewall systems, Web services, browser applications, data recovery systems, and more are affected by upgrades. All of these change at frequent intervals, and that is just the way it is. It is out of your control.

The management issue is to be sure that the computer operations staff have an ongoing benchmarking process so that any unintended changes are spotted early by staff rather than later by a patient, vendor, or payer. This is different from "testing before use" because the changes happen without notice. The benchmarking process is your only hope for knowing whether the system is working the way you think it is.

Data input is always an issue with computer applications. Hand input is unreliable. Voice input is getting better, but it is still several generations away from being accurate enough to count on. Electronic input, such as barcode scanning, is quite good. Biometrics, which includes fingerprint, retina, face, and voice scanners, is coming along, but each of these has its own practical difficulties in the healthcare environment. Good system design feeds the input back to the worker for confirmation prior to commitment, and the same good system design allows the worker to recognize and correct any problems on the spot.

Willful Misconduct

And so we return to worker error. This time, we are discussing willful misconduct, dereliction of duty, substance abuse, sabotage, or a prank gone awry. This is not a matter of task design, this is a matter of an employee who wants to be an ex-employee.

Nothing weakens staff respect for management so quickly and thoroughly as a manifest ineptitude when it comes to dealing with problem employees, and this is deservedly so. Take care of the situation. Get rid of problem employees. Get rid of problem managers, too.

Solutions

Seek a particular solution, and seek a general solution. The general solution usually requires management action.

Generalizing the Solution

After management is confident that it has identified the chain of events and the causes of the event, it needs to be sure that a solution is provided that definitively covers the particular event and, in addition, covers the general class of events exemplified by the particular case. Finding that general solution usually falls to management because it almost always involves a change in policy, a change in technology, or a change in capital facilities.

A change in technology has the advantage that it can be given a trial run, and any concomitant issues can be seen and addressed. Changes in policy are hard to implement on a trial-run basis; the change either is the new policy or it is not the new policy. It is also hard to make changes in a capital facility on a trial basis. Once the concrete is poured, it is a little late to discover and fix awkward features of the new facility. One possibility is to do the trial somewhere else. Find a similar organization that has already established the new policy or built a comparable facility. Visit it, scrutinize it, and dig out the anecdotes as well as the facts and figures.

Caution

No solution is ever guaranteed. Every change in an organization, whether it is a policy change, a technology change, or a capital facility change, needs to be done with a great deal of care and caution. Managing change is a key facet of Six Sigma, and it is covered later in this book.

Positive Applications

Not all events are bad; some are surprisingly good. The same management approach that gets you to an understanding of an untoward event and its causes will work just as well with a positive event. Applying this systematically to positive events is a sound way to improve overall performance. This may even be considered management of serendipity.

Benefit from Creativity

1. Encourage
2. Observe
3. Be curious
4. Understand
5. Capitalize

Most scientific discoveries are made this way—not by accident exactly but by seizing on fortunate happenings. Being observant is the second requisite; being curious is the third. Being ready to follow up and dig in to understand what is causing the favorable result is the fourth benefit.

Any organization may have employees who are creative in their work. They find easier ways to do things to save themselves some time and effort. This is not cutting corners, it is creativity.

Management has the responsibility of encouraging responsible creativity at all levels for the simple reason that management does not have the energy or the opportunity to do all the creative work itself. Help from all ranks is to be appreciated.

When the Six Sigma management system is mature in an organization, all key processes are tracked. From the tracking charts, it is just as easy to see a favorable event as an unfavorable event. The unfavorable events have their own way of demanding attention. Management is responsible for paying attention to the favorable events, too.

DIAGRAMMATIC TOOLS

Failure Modes and Effects Analysis

The idea of the failure modes and effects analysis is to link events, usually without much consideration of the likelihood of any particular event or combination of events. More elaborate forms include probabilistic weighting, but that is beyond what is likely to be needed for management purposes in dealing with some untoward event, either real or hypothetical.

The failure modes and effects analysis can be done from effects back to causes or from causes forward to effects. For example, consider this effect: a wheel comes off the mail cart. What can cause this? The wheel itself could break, the cart leg could break, the axle could break, the cotter pin could come out of the axle, or the shank of the leg down where the axle goes through it could get bent so that the axle could pop out. We could then go further back to ask, what would cause the axle to break? Well, the answer may be poor lubrication, material defect, destructive handling during assembly, abrasion against the strut, chemical attack by disinfectant used to wash the cart, and so on. Similar lists could be developed for each of the other causes of the wheel coming off.

FIGURE 5: FAILURE MODES AND EFFECTS ANALYSIS EXAMPLE

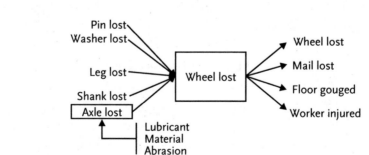

The Six Sigma Book for Healthcare

Alternatively we could go in the other direction and ask, what happens if the wheel comes off? Well, the cart might tip, mail could be dumped on the floor, mail would be held up, some mail might get lost, the aisle could be blocked by the wreckage, the cart user might be injured by the spill, another cart going by might be tipped in turn, the floor might get gouged, or a passerby might get a pocketful of mail.

These types of diagrams are commonly drawn out in a tree. Before computers came along, they were drawn on the back of wallpaper rolls. They can be done by hand on a blackboard if the exercise is restricted to likely events and significant consequences.

It may be helpful to ask the following:

1. How is this supposed to work?
2. Where are the obvious weak spots at which something might fail?
3. If failure transpires, what are the consequences?
4. If such consequences are significant, can some change be proposed to mitigate those particular consequences?

If some change is proposed, restart the process and think again through weak spots, failure modes, and consequences.

Predicting every eventuality is impossible. Reasonable effort should be put into thinking the situation through, looking for potential problems, and thinking about failure modes and effects, but those will never replace some actual experience (mostly likely experience acquired in a trial run).

NASA has lost, sad to say, a small number of astronauts in the past 40 years; each was lost in an accident. In no case had that accident been foreseen in a prior failure modes and effects analysis, even though NASA had committed to such analyses to an exhaustive degree precisely in an effort to preclude the loss of astronauts. NASA's failure modes and effects analysis work, with an unlimited budget, was not and could not have been 100 percent complete. The proof of this is that the analysis was done, designs were improved to preclude loss, and a few astronauts were lost anyway. The point is this: failure modes and effects analyses are tools to be used, but they are not the totality of the problem-solving effort.

Even with these limitations, failure modes and effects analysis will focus attention on ripple effects and provide an organized means to identify and preclude a large portion of the ripples beforehand. A complementary method known as potential problem analysis will be discussed later.

Fishbone Analysis

The existing system got the way it is for various good reasons over the life of the organization. Certainly these reasons seemed pretty solid at the time the existing management policy was put in place. Changing things now will work best if the decision-making process includes an understanding of how things got the way they are.

Informing the affected parties is a pretty good policy. Getting input from these parties is also a pretty good policy. Getting input from various ranks in the organization is, again, a pretty good policy. These policies are to be weighed against the likelihood of reinventing the present system or of running out of time to do anything.

A useful tool to apply at the gathering-views stage is the fishbone diagram, which is also called an Ishikawa diagram. This tool is useful in gathering and organizing input without applying any judgment to the value of the input, at least not while the diagram is being made. In other words, this tool is useful in defusing meetings by getting everybody's input onto one chart. Part of the input is very likely to be a discussion of why the present system is the way it is. This is informative for the rest of the group, and it may give rise to better suggestions for improvement.

A suitable candidate for change is one that deals with one or more of the issues on the fishbone diagram. To put it another way, unless the change candidate deals with one or more of the issues on the fishbone diagram, the change is not going to make any difference.

The fishbone diagram is not a chain of events, and it does not distinguish very well among mechanisms, conditions, and constraints. This is okay; it is still a good place to start. The information can be sorted out later onto the three-plane model.

Here is an example of a fishbone diagram that looks at the various possible causes of delay in getting a patient transferred by cart from one patient care unit to a different patient care unit.

FIGURE 6: FISHBONE DIAGRAM EXAMPLE

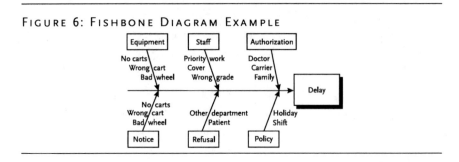

The fishbone diagram itself does not prioritize anything or give more weight to one item than to another. The point, at this stage of the analysis, is to be inclusive.

MANAGEMENT ACTION

If it is immediately obvious that new policy will solve the problem forever-more, management should institute that policy. This, unfortunately, is almost never the case. Sorting out issues, considering alternatives, think-ing things through, and testing the best candidates for new policies takes time and effort. Therefore, management needs to proceed in a step-by-step fashion:

1. Institute a stop-gap measure to break the chain(s) of events.
2. Authorize a study group to consider the chain(s) of events, the circumstances, and the policies now in force and to propose new policies.
3. Expect the study group to do fishbone diagrams and other cause and effect fact gathering and information gathering.
4. Expect the study group to identify the chain(s) of events.
5. Expect the study group to apply the three-plane model.
6. Expect the study group to recommend new constraints in the form of new management policies or actions.
7. Authorize a trial of the proposed new policies.
8. Evaluate the trial.
9. Apply the new policy in a general way if the trial is successful.
10. Monitor results on a long-term basis to be confident that circum-stances have not changed in some adverse way over time.

The "policy change" is quite often a technology change, which is to say that the new policy is to use technology X rather than the prior technology Y. Such decisions may require substantial funding and may take time to implement. Meanwhile, the stop-gap measures must be kept in place.

The policy and/or technology change needs to be tested carefully in a trial before it is applied universally. How to manage the trial will be discussed later in this book.

Joint Commission Sentinel Events

The Joint Commission mandates specific actions for sentinel events (Joint Commission 2001). A Joint Commission sentinel event, then, is a manifestation of a problem that needs to be solved. The Six Sigma method for problem solving conforms to the Joint Commission requirements for analyzing and preventing the reoccurrence of sentinel events. This method is not restricted to such serious matters as sentinel events; the same systematic method can be applied to both great matters and small matters. Indeed, having some experience with small and medium-sized matters is good preparation before having to deal with a life-threatening event.

Joint Commission Root-Cause Analysis

Root-cause analysis is a process for identifying the basic or causal factors that underlie variation in performance, including the occurrence or possible occurrence of a sentinel event. A root-cause analysis focuses primarily on systems and processes rather than on individual performance. It progresses from special causes in clinical processes to common causes in organizational processes and identifies potential improvements in processes or systems that would tend to decrease the likelihood of such events in the future. Alternatively, it determines that, after analysis, no such improvement opportunities can be found to exist.

Note: Used with permission of the Joint Commission

JOINT COMMISSION SENTINEL EVENTS

A sentinel event is an unexpected occurrence involving death, serious physical or psychological injury, or the risk thereof. Serious injury specifically includes loss of limb or function. The phrase "or the risk thereof" includes any process variation for which a reoccurrence would carry a significant chance of a serious adverse outcome.

Such events are called "sentinel" because they signal the need for immediate investigation and response.

Expectations under the standards for an organization's response to a sentinel event are as follows:

1. Accredited organizations are expected to identify and respond appropriately to *all* sentinel events occurring in the organization or associated with services the organization provides or provides for.
2. Appropriate response includes conducting a timely, thorough, and credible root-cause analysis, implementing improvements to reduce risk, and monitoring the effectiveness of those improvements.

Note: Used with permission of the Joint Commission.

Root Causes

The Joint Commission has a specific definition of root causes that it wishes to see applied in analyses done for sentinel events. The general notion is that pulling out the cause at its root solves the problem for good. However, this presupposes that the root cause can be found, something can be done about it, and that something is within the control of the organization's management. None of these is necessarily true.

Three-plane analysis is useful in seeking root causes. Sometimes the root cause is merely a breakdown in the mechanism, which is cured by replacing or upgrading the mechanism. More often, the root cause is found on the conditions plane, and dealing with the root cause—pulling the root out—requires some management action toward change, and this will show up on the constraints plane.

Here are a few examples:

Condition	Constraint
Patients move around of their own volition, including wandering off the premises.	Change policy to restrict movement past the property line, and reinforce it with alarm technology.
Visitors carry newborn babies out of the maternity rooms.	Change policy to restrict the movement of babies by visitors to same-room.
Employees carry laptop computers home to do extra work. Some computers get lost.	Change policy to require any such employees to carry insurance against such loss.

Breaking a chain of events is different from pulling out a root cause. Take the example cited in the conditions/constraints table above dealing with employees who take computers home to do additional work. There is a way to break the chain of events: forbid employees from taking computers home. However, if the employee cannot take the computer home, he or she is not going to do that report, special assignment, or self-help study, and the organization surely wants to encourage all of those things. Perhaps requiring the employee to carry insurance against loss of the organization's computers is a better solution, even if the organization gives the employee money to cover the additional insurance cost. Perhaps better solutions or different constraints could address the condition, protect the organization's interests, and avoid discouraging employees from doing extra work outside of the office.

The mechanisms leading to a specific event are themselves quite specific—so specific in fact that breaking the chain of events probably only precludes that specific event from happening again. Other events of the same class may still happen because their mechanics are slightly different. To find a more general solution (to pull the root cause), looking at the conditions and constraints, which are general, not specific, is appropriate.

Problem Detection

Detecting abnormal conditions before they become problems is better than waiting for untoward events to happen.

Problem detection requires that a baseline be established and quantified, that ongoing data be gathered and tracked, and that warning levels be established so that abnormal data can be flagged and studied in detail.

Management may become aware of abnormal conditions through anecdotal reports. Taking action to correct such conditions usually works better if quantitative information is in hand.

SIX SIGMA MEASURES

For ongoing operations, we will measure the overall system error rate and the variability of the error rate. Because most organizations provide several treatments or services, keeping track of error rates and variability for each makes sense. We will also most often be interested in the error rate for each work unit involved in each service and its variability. As a measure of variability, we will track the standard deviation of each item of interest.

We will commonly keep track of the time duration involved in each step and its variability. There is no Six Sigma goal for variability, but tracking variability is important because the variability plays into the ongoing analysis of each process.

Six Sigma organizations seek to perform at an error rate of 3.4 errors per million opportunities. How many opportunities for error does a healthcare service organization encounter? For present purposes, assume that a professional employee does something five to ten times an hour, each attempt of which might go wrong or might be delayed. For every 100 professional employees, that equates to one to two million opportunities for error in a year. Nonprofessionals, being more task-oriented, would likely have 15 to 30 opportunities per hour. Every 100 nonprofessionals, then, would have three to six million opportunities for error per year.

That said, an organization of 500 people, with 150 professionals and 350 nonprofessionals, would have about one to two million opportunities for error per month. If this organization were applying Six Sigma successfully, the number of errors for the whole organization would be less than ten per month. Even a very good organization operating in the best known mode will still have errors cropping up because having perfection in service is not possible by any known means. However, those rare errors will be found and corrected promptly in an ongoing, managed way.

How Are We Doing?

America Today

Industry: Four sigma

Services: One to two sigma

(Breyfogle, Cupello, and Meadows 2001)

Studies show that American industry is presently running at about four sigma and that service organizations are running at one to two sigma (Breyfogle, Cupello, and Meadows 2001). How big is a sigma? What does "four sigma" or "one to two sigma" performance mean?

The symbol σ, or sigma, represents the standard deviation of a distribution of possible occurrences. The most familiar distribution is the normal distribution, which is that familiar, bell-shaped curve. The normal curve is plotted against the number of standard deviations; it is symmetric in relation to its average value. The normal curve is one of those curves that never quite gets to zero: no matter how far along the sigma-axis one goes, a little more tail continues to the right, and the same is true for the left side of the curve, which is for the negative values of sigma. Sometimes both tails are of interest, and sometimes only one side or the other is.

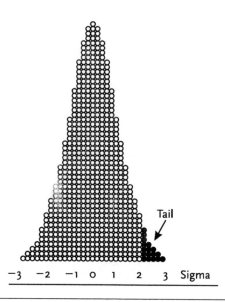

The present matter of interest is how much of a tail corresponds to a particular sigma value. The tail is the area under the normal curve to the right of the sigma value. To show some specific numbers, here are the tails for a selection of sigma values.

Sigma Value	Tail	
	Items per 1,000	Items per Million
1	159	158,665
2	23	22,750
3	1	1,350
4		32
4.5		3.4

A system running at the one-sigma level experiences 159 errors per 1,000 opportunities, a system running at the two-sigma level experiences 23 errors per 1,000 opportunities, and a system running at the three-sigma level experiences about 1 error per 1,000 opportunities.

For higher sigma values, it is more convenient to present the number of errors per million opportunities. A system running at the three-sigma level is experiencing 1,350 errors per million, a system running at the four-sigma level experiences 32 errors per million, and a system running at the 4.5-sigma level experiences 3.4 errors per million.

Six Sigma organizations want to be so sure that the 3.4 errors per million goal is met that, rather than setting 4.5 sigma as the goal, the bar is set at a full six sigma; this allows 1.5 sigma for process variation. Process variation may arise from normal turnover in work crews, the time needed to gain familiarity with new equipment, the addition of new services, and the like. Making some allowance for such common process variations is considered more prudent than having to explain shortfalls later on.

Returning to our hypothetical healthcare organization with 500 employees, the number of opportunities for error is one to two million per month, so the number of errors for the organization per month would be as follows:

Sigma	Organization Errors per Month	
	Low	High
1	158,000	317,000
2	22,750	45,500
3	1,350	2,700
4	32	63
4.5	3.4	6.8

If service organizations are running between one and two sigma these days, then our 500-person organization would be experiencing perhaps 100,000 errors per month. That is a lot; it is about 200 errors per person per month, or about one error per person every hour.

Suppose our organization is better than average: it is running at 2.5 sigma, which would be about 10,000 errors per month, which can also be stated as 20 errors per person per month or about one error per person per day. On the other hand, if our organization were achieving 4.5 sigma, the entire organization would be making about five errors per month, which would be 0.01 errors per person, or one error per person every eight years or so.

The improvement for our hypothetical organization would be from several thousand errors per month to fewer than ten per month. The improvement would be reflected directly in improved service to patients and in a direct reduction in the cost, capacity, and management effort presently applied to correcting errors and dealing with the consequences of errors.

Even if as few as one or two errors per person per day occur, it is not difficult to imagine that 10 percent of the total effort goes into correcting mistakes. If the organization is presently putting 10 percent of its resources into error and the consequences of error, the organization stands to recover nearly all of that misapplication of its resources, and that savings goes directly to the bottom line.

We have said that an error is any departure from specification. Suppose the specification is that a service department perform on a particular time schedule, with a time window specified. Failure to perform within this time window counts as an error. Suppose certain laboratory reports are part of a healthcare service and that the system is set up to tolerate report turnaround with an average of four hours and a range from three to five hours. Timely delivery of these reports is important to the completion of the patient's care; anything earlier causes confusion, and anything later causes delays.

On the left-hand side of the figure below, the laboratory is meeting the requirement and honoring the established service window in time. This meets the Crosby definition of quality because the specification is met.

FIGURE 8: INCONSISTENT AND CONSISTENT PERFORMANCE

Arrival Times

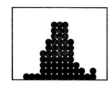

Arrival Times

On the right-hand side of the figure, the laboratory is doing a little more by delivering the reports on a consistent basis very near the nominal average delivery time. This meets the Crosby definition, and it also does something more: it meets the requirements with great consistency. Meeting specifications with consistency is an embellishment on the Crosby quality requirement that was expanded by Taguchi (1978), and it is a good goal to keep in mind.

If one had the choice, one would certainly choose to appear on the right-hand side of the figure, the side that represents consistent performance. With that level of performance, the receiving department will have more confidence that the next report will arrive within the time window.

SIX SIGMA OPERATIONS ANALYSIS

System Yield and Performance Time

Multistep Performance

The overall yield is the product of the yields of each of the steps.

The overall performance time is the sum of the performance times of each of the steps.

The yield is the ratio of desired outcomes to total outcomes.

The system yield is the ratio of the number of everything-right-the-first-time patients to the total number of patients treated. The system yield is also the product of the yields of each step in the overall process.

The system performance time is the time needed to complete the treatment and discharge the patient. The system performance time is also the sum of the treatment times of each step in the overall process plus any waiting time.

The system yield has an average value and a standard deviation; so does the system performance time. Most healthcare organizations provide more than one service, so there would be a yield and a performance time for each of them.

Example One

Suppose the system yield is 99.9 percent and the system performance time is 50 hours. That means the next patient could expect to move through the system in about 50 hours. Out of the next 1,000 patients, *one* can expect to require corrective action to overcome some error made inside the system. The number of patients in the system getting corrective action would be a tiny fraction of the whole patient population. This is good because resources devoted to that corrective action are resources that are not available for taking care of the next patient.

Example Two

Suppose now that the overall system yield is found to be 80 percent with a standard deviation of 3 percent, and suppose that the overall system performance time is found to be 100 hours with a standard deviation of 5 hours.

Any single patient can expect to be through the system in about 100 hours. Only one patient out of 1,000 will expect to take longer than 115 hours (the arithmetic will be developed in the following sections), and a few out of a million will take longer than 130 hours. These are patients who require no corrective action during the overall process; they are simply held up someplace along the line for more time than the average.

Because the yield is only 80 percent, a 20 percent chance exists that any one patient will be held up for additional work and that, out of several groups of patients, some groups may see as many as 29 percent of the group held up for additional work. In extremely rare cases, a group may see as many as 38 percent held up for additional work.

Clearly, having 20 percent of patients being given additional treatment means that a lot of the effort of the system is being given over to this additional corrective care. If this additional care involves the bottleneck of the system, the overall capacity of the system is reduced directly by this fraction. Therefore, management efforts to improve the yield at each process step will be rewarded by reducing the effort going into that additional care, and the capacity of the overall system will increase as less additional work flows through the bottleneck.

Example Three

The average treatment time is not known, and the yield is not known. Everybody seems happy, though, and nothing seems to get stuck in the middle. This is a good situation to leave alone. There are bound to be greater difficulties elsewhere.

Example Four

The average treatment time is not known, and the yield is not known. Complaints are coming in about work being redone, about work or patients piling up, and about unhappy employees. This scenario goes on the list for further examination. Something is wrong, and the management might as well find out what it is now rather than finding out the hard way later. It is best to gather information and organize it so that informed decisions can be reached.

Six Sigma Process Analysis

Six Sigma provides an organized way of gathering and organizing information about ongoing processes by proceeding step by step:

1. Select key or troublesome processes.
2. Quantify present performance to have a baseline.
3. Evaluate candidate changes to improve the process.
4. Execute process improvements on a trial basis.
5. Extend successful trials to the organization.
6. Monitor the new process over the long term.
7. Select the next candidates for improvement.

There will always be another candidate process worthy of consideration because technology changes, the services that are offered change, personnel change, and outside factors come into play, such as new regulations. Therefore, Six Sigma becomes an abiding feature of organizations that take up Six Sigma and find it to be effective.

Six Sigma performance begins by gathering and organizing information. On the basis of this information, changes are considered and given a trial run in controlled circumstances. If these trials are successful, the change can be implemented widely. The ongoing monitoring that follows ensures that no deterioration goes undetected over time. In addition, the ongoing monitoring may bring to light some pattern of performance that is better than usual and that deserves closer attention as a potential benefit.

Six Sigma System Limits

Each process' yield and duration have two characteristics: an average and a standard deviation. These two characteristics become the basis for quantitative analysis of the process.

The Six Sigma method establishes two *system limits* for each process: the upper system limit and the lower system limit. The system limits bracket the process outcomes from above and below and the space in between is called the system limits band or just the system band.

To make use of these, we will use tracking charts and plot data points on these charts against time. We will draw a horizontal line to represent the average value, and we will draw the system limits six standard deviations away from the average value.

A process governed by a normal distribution will take on values more than 4.5 standard deviations away from the average only 3.4 times in a million. (See the appendix for consideration of the small error that results from using the normal distribution where a discrete distribution would be justified. Using the normal distribution is more convenient, even at a cost of a small loss of precision.) Because that is the numerical goal for Six Sigma, the logic for allowing 4.5 standard deviations of room for random fluctuations is easy to see. Six Sigma goes beyond this by allowing an additional 1.5 standard deviations for drift in the process average value. Adding 4.5 and 1.5 standard deviations gives six standard deviations. The system limits are drawn six standard deviations away from the average value; this is done separately for the process yield and the process duration. If the lower limit goes below zero, it is set to zero. (See the appendix for consideration of the small error resulting from ignoring negative values.)

To see the reason for the additional 1.5 standard deviations of allowance, consider that it is prudent to allow some measure for the aging of equipment, variations in the weather, bringing new people into the work group, a change in suppliers, and every other ordinary reason that might come along. The system limits are pretty important, and changes in them may cause ripples throughout the organization, so allow some leeway for these nonspecific influences to be on the safe side. The size of the allowance is open for debate; American industry has found that an allowance of 1.5 standard deviations seems to be practical, and so it has been adopted as part of the Six Sigma method.

To demonstrate this, below is a chart showing a typical normal distribution with the 3.4-per-million limits shown at plus and minus 4.5 standard deviations from the average value and the system limits marked at plus and minus 6 standard deviations.

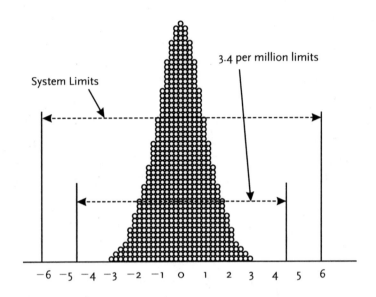

This normal distribution, as long as it stays where it is in the middle of the system band, will have fluctuations that reach the system limits much less often than 3.4 times per million because there is substantial white space between the 3.4-per-million limits and the system limits.

In the next chart, the process, for some as-yet-unknown reason, has drifted somewhat to the right by about one standard deviation. The 3.4-per-million limits move with the distribution because they are simply characteristics of that distribution. The system limits, however, do not; once they are set, they stay the same. In this case, because of the drift, the white space has largely been eaten up on the right-hand side. Although it may well be time to take action to rectify the situation, the built-in allowance provides a margin so that the system limits are not yet violated more than 3.4 times per million.

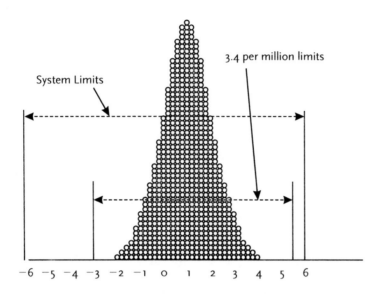

Why System Limits Are Important

The system limits for a process are a declaration to the overall system that says, "This is what I can do with great reliability. If you ask no more of me than this, I can perform to Six Sigma standards. If you ask more, I will likely fail to meet the Six Sigma standards. If you want tighter system limits, you will have to change the process."

The system limits are the interface between this process and the organization. Suppose the process in question is the x-ray department, and suppose that observations lead to the determination that the average time to provide an x-ray, once the patient is delivered to the x-ray department door, is 30 minutes with a standard deviation of five minutes. The upper system limit for x-ray completion time comes to $30 + (6 * 5) = 60$ minutes. The patient care unit requesting the x-ray would need to plan sufficiently to allow for as much as 60 minutes for the x-ray to not be disappointed more than 3.4 times per million. Of the 60 minutes, 7.5 minutes are the white-space allowance for process drift over time.

The patient care unit would likely demand that the x-ray department pay attention and turn patients around a good deal more promptly than that, to which the x-ray department can say, "Yes, we would like to do better and we will consider ways to do better, but that is the process that exists today, and we do not know how to improve it overnight, so you had better plan on 60 minutes until further notice."

Knowing the system limits provides a basis for rational management action at three places. Higher management can see the benefit of capital improvements or additional staffing in the x-ray department because it will have an observable benefit in treatment time. The x-ray department itself has a rational basis for putting forward capital and staffing requests. The patient care unit has a rational basis for planning its work to a reliable schedule.

Suppose the measure is not of x-ray completion time but rather of the incidence of lost x-rays, which result in the patient having to be returned to the x-ray department to be x-rayed again. If that happens frequently, the x-ray department must have the capacity to deal with the reshoots, the patient care unit must plan for the likelihood of reshoots, and the whole treatment process must make a suitable allowance. Having the system limits established provides a basis for deciding what to do in each of the affected units.

Process Tracking

Establishing the system limits once does not end the necessary interest in each process. Things change, so it is important to keep track of performance over time. The system limits are set so wide that they will not likely ever be violated in the normal course of events; indeed, that is the whole point. Therefore, it is generally helpful to establish an additional pair of limits, for tracking purposes, that are closer to where the data points are expected to fall.

The customary way of doing this is to set limits at plus and minus three standard deviations, which will be surpassed about one time in every 1,000. Crossing these lines does not violate anything; it simply puts the responsible people on notice that something unusual has happened. Maybe it is a random fluctuation, or maybe it is something going awry in the process. It is a data point worth some additional attention.

Limits set at plus and minus three standard deviations have the historical name of "process control limits," although nothing is being controlled in the usual sense of the word. (Nothing is "controlled" at a border passport control office either, so using the word in this sense, to mean inspection or observation, is not unique.) When data points fall outside the process control limits, the mechanisms for problem solving, which were described earlier, can be applied. When data points fall outside the system limits, those mechanisms certainly should be applied.

A Pharmacy Order Example

Consider this hypothetical case. A hospital has a pharmacy, and the pharmacy fills medication orders from the patient care units. Experience shows that about one medication order in 1,000 is wrong; either the dosage level is wrong or the drug delivered is not the one intended. Management is concerned about this level of performance and decides to take action; an additional rechecking step is initiated to break the chain of events. Then management decides that additional information should be gathered so that an informed decision can be made regarding permanent changes in the system.

Closer analysis of the data shows that the error rate is one per 1,000 over a 20-month period and that the error rate in some months is higher and in some months lower. The order flow diagram at this point is about like this:

FIGURE 11: PHARMACY ORDER, INITIAL MODEL

The error rate per 1,000 orders is found to be the following, as tabulated by month:

Month	Error Rate per 1,000	Month	Error Rate per 1,000
June	2.1	May	1.1
July	0.4	June	0.3
August	0.6	July	1.3
September	1.7	August	1.5
October	0.4	September	1.3
November	0.5	October	1.2
December	0	November	0.5
January	1.0	December	1.2
February	0.2	January	0.6
March	1.4	**Average**	**1.0**
April	2.1	**Standard Deviation**	**0.8**

The tabulated data show that the average error rate is 1 error per 1,000 orders; the standard deviation is found to be 0.8 per 1,000 orders. These are easily calculated with any spreadsheet application. For example, the Excel® built-in functions are AVERAGE(. . .) and STDEV(. . .).

FIGURE 12: PHARMACY ERROR HISTOGRAM AND SYSTEM LIMITS

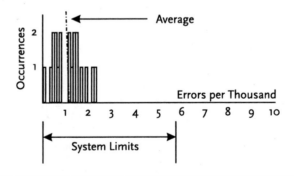

A histogram of the data helps to visualize what is going on. The histogram above presents the data in a particular graphical form that shows the frequency with which each error rate occurs. The x-axis is divided into conveniently small steps. For example, in this figure, the step size is one-tenth of an error per 1,000. Bigger or smaller steps can be tried until a reasonable graph presents itself.

The average rate of occurrence is one per 1,000, which we already knew, and some bunching of the data appears near the average value, which seems to be reasonable. The maximum observed error rate is between two errors and three errors per 1,000; one would be tempted to say that somehow allowing for three errors per 1,000 would sufficiently cover the situation.

However, because the number of observations is small, it is necessary to allow for a higher error rate to cover the range of fluctuations that happen with a normal distribution. That is where Six Sigma comes in. System limits will be drawn at plus and minus six standard deviations. The lower system limit is set at zero because errors cannot occur a negative number of times. The upper system limit is set six standard deviations above the average, which comes to 5.8 errors per 1,000. With these system limits, which include an allowance for process drift, the likelihood of exceeding the upper limit is not greater than 3.4 per million.

What does this mean? This means that the present pharmacy order process cannot be relied on to have an error rate of less than 5.8 per 1,000 orders. Thus the situation is worse than management originally thought. True, the average error rate is 1 per 1,000, but the error rate may rise as high as 5.8 per 1,000 just from random fluctuations plus an allowance for process drift. Management actions are in order.

First, the stop-gap measure of additional checking would be continued indefinitely. Second, the standard treatment schedule would be changed to allow an extra period of time to get a replacement pharmacy order filled on an expedited basis for those cases in which the rechecking turns up an error in the pharmacy order.

The revised flow chart might look something like this:

FIGURE 13: REVISED PHARMACY ORDER SYSTEM

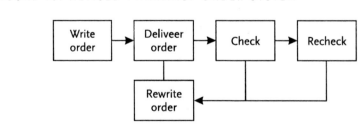

With the stop-gap procedure in place, management could set about studying and changing the system to reduce both the average error rate and the variation in error rate, considering such system changes as penmanship lessons, computer-terminal order entry, computer cross-checking for standard dosages, and computer cross-checking against the patient record. One or more of these would be tested on a trial basis, and when a successful system change is found and validated, the organization would ideally switch over to the better system.

Understanding the Baseline

When a target process is selected, the first step to take is to gather information about how the system works currently in and around this target. This becomes the baseline against which future changes can be measured.

For the work done by the target activity or activities, are average completion times and standard deviations known? Have process control limits been calculated? Are completion times tracked? What happens if the work is done incorrectly and has to be repeated? How does that show up in the tracking record?

Every process—every system—has some variability. A key to applying Six Sigma is to *accept* that the process has some variability; this variability is a characteristic of the process and cannot be removed or reduced without changing the nature of the process. Attempting to reduce the variability by interceding in the process will only increase the variability.

In a factory, the speed of the machines determines capacity. In a service organization, management is tempted to believe that more can be done if people would just work harder, pay more attention, think ahead, hurry up, or follow orders more diligently. We do not expect machines to work faster, but we do expect humans to work faster—with no limit. This is not rational, but it seems to be true.

However, the employees are probably working about as productively as they can in the current system. Maybe a hurry-up campaign will work, briefly, once in a while, but no sustained result is likely to flow from hurry-up exhortation.

It is more useful—and part of the Six Sigma concept—to start with the view that each employee is working productively and that, if an employee is slow or making errors, he or she may need additional training or a different work setup. Straightforward analysis and corrective action on the local level is the best way to solve the particular problem and build a platform for the future.

What type of analysis is likely to help? We will now take a look at some useful tools.

Process Flow Diagrams

A process flow diagram is a chart that helps management understand what is going on; it may also help participants from diverse departments to understand what is going on. The chart may even help the knowledgeable participants to understand more fully what is going on because they may never have thought about things in just the way they were presented in the chart.

Process flow charts can get out of hand very quickly if the level of detail is not adjusted to a productive level. It is better to have a family of charts than to put everything onto one. These are sometimes called the "50,000-foot view," the "1,000-foot view," and the "10-foot view."

A process flow chart for the x-ray patient above would be something on the order of this:

FIGURE 14: X-RAY VISIT PROCESS FLOW CHART

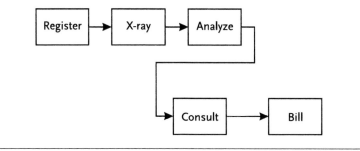

The process flow chart usually shows only the value-adding steps, not the in-between waits. For Six Sigma analysis, a process flow chart is of some value, but the time-value diagram is of more value because it gets to the heart of a key issue. The process flow chart may be thought of as an introductory chart to get to the time-value chart.

Process flow charts are easily produced by such computer applications as VISIO® and SMARTDRAW®. They can also be drawn, with a little more effort, directly in a word processing document or spreadsheet using the primitive textbox and arrow-drawing tools provided.

Control Charts

Consider the following data, which will represent the delivery times of x-ray results over a calendar week.

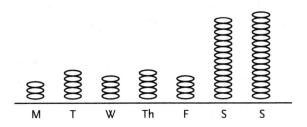

FIGURE 15: SEVEN DAYS OF DATA, HISTOGRAM

Clearly some different activity is transpiring on Saturday and Sunday; this is a system issue. Exhortation is not likely to improve weekend performance much, because a mismatch is likely between workload and staff or staff skills. More legwork is in order to gain a better understanding of the problem.

Look now at the variability during the Monday through Friday period. The count is not uniform: it is three, five, four, five, and four, respectively. This is the inherent variability of the process. This is what the system can do and does today. The variability is not very great—only one or two counts from day to day—but it is not zero; some variability is inherent in the daily level.

The counts are characterized by a *chronic* variability level, which is three to five units per day in the case at hand, and an *episodic* level that occurs on Saturday and Sunday, which is an additional count of about six units per day.

Suppose on a Monday the count is two. Does that show improvement? Suppose on the following day, a Tuesday, the count is six. Does that show a collapse in the system? In both cases, the answer is no. A count of two or six once in a while can be expected because of the inherent, chronic variability in the process.

Here is how to figure out what the limits on reasonable expectations are for the chronic variability in the process:

Ignore the weekend data and consider only the weekday data, where the chronic variability is easy to see.

Use a spreadsheet computer application, enter the weekday data into the spreadsheet, and use the built-in functions to calculate the average value and the standard deviation of the data set. In Microsoft Excel®, the functions are AVERAGE(. . .) and STDEV(. . .). Other spreadsheet products might have slightly different names for these functions, but they all have them.

Here is how the spreadsheet should look:

Day	Count
Monday	3
Tuesday	5
Wednesday	4
Thursday	5
Friday	4
Average	4.2
Standard deviation	0.84
Three times the standard deviation	2.51

Having a simple, graphic way of knowing what process variation is to be expected is useful. This can be done by drawing lines at the average plus/minus three standard deviations levels because a normal distribution stays within plus/minus three standard deviations 99.7 percent of the time. Data points may show up outside these limits, but they are so unlikely that they deserve special scrutiny every time. If the data points stay within these limits, everything can be considered to be working the way it is expected to work given the system as it currently exists.

These limits are called "process control limits," even though no particular control is being applied:

Upper control limit = Average + Three standard deviations

Lower control limit = Average − Three standard deviations

Variations that fall within this control band can be considered normal variations. Variations that fall outside this band can be considered abnormal, and they call for special attention. They are probably *not* naturally occurring.

This can be monitored simply by creating a process control chart, which has the ongoing results and two lines showing the upper and lower control limit lines. The process control chart shown above would take on this look:

FIGURE 16: PROCESS CONTROL CHART BASED ON FIVE DAYS

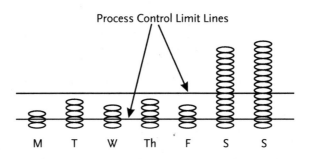

A quick look at this process control chart tells us that something odd is going on over the weekend. We already knew that, so it is comforting that the analysis confirms it.

So far, the weekend data have been considered as departures from the nominal system. However, if these data must be included because there is no way to deal with them using separate management policies or other distinct actions, the analysis would need to include all seven days of data.

Repeat the Excel® spreadsheet calculations to include seven days' data:

Day	Count
Monday	3
Tuesday	5
Wednesday	4
Thursday	5
Friday	4
Saturday	14
Sunday	15
Average	7.14
Standard deviation	5.08
Three times the standard deviation	15.24

In this case, the lower control chart limit is negative, which has no physical meaning and can be set to zero. This happens because the normal distribution, used for convenience, is not the perfect representation for the data. However, little practical benefit comes from searching for a better representation in most real cases, and the practical effect is negligible (see appendix).

FIGURE 17: PROCESS CONTROL CHART BASED ON SEVEN DAYS

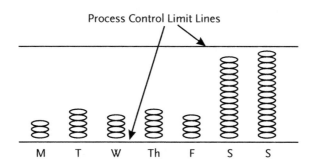

Including the weekend data makes a big difference in both the average value and the standard deviation. As shown in the two tables above, the standard deviation estimate changed from 0.84 to 5.08, a change of 4.24 units. The wider process control band now encompasses all of the data points on the diagram because all of the points have been accepted as normal points.

The name for this kind of chart, "process control chart," may give the impression that something is being controlled and that the data points are being forced to stay within the control band; this is not the case. The process control limits are characteristics of the process as it presently exists. Nothing is being controlled in the usual meaning of the word.

The value of the process control limits is that any data point falling outside of the control band is an unusual data point (one that would occur only about once per 1,000 events) if the process that is being tracked is still running the way it was when the process control lines were drawn. Any point outside the lines may be all right, but chances are something exceptional is happening. Any point outside the process control limit lines should get close scrutiny. Furthermore, if a pattern develops in which several points fall outside the lines, the process has changed and something is wrong.

For this tracking purpose alone, the process control chart makes good practice for every process in the system that impinges on service. These charts are easy to make and easy to understand, and they have direct meaning for service management.

Six Sigma System Limit Lines

In addition to the process control lines, Six Sigma adds two more lines: the system limit lines. The space between the system limit lines is called the system limit band. The system limit lines are drawn six standard deviations away from the process average, so the system limit band is twice as wide as the process control band. Six Sigma also requires that the process average be no closer to either system limit than 4.5 times the process average value; this may happen if the process drifts or is changed in some way. Normal process variability will produce points outside of the system limits only a few times in a million events.

The system limits constitute a conceptual fence between this process and the overall system. The process agrees to keep itself within the system limits, and the system agrees not to demand anything from the system beyond staying within the system limits. If the organization wants more performance from this process, some change has to be made to improve the process so that the system limit band can be contracted.

The Management Interest

Note that the level of management interest is different between the process control limits and the system limits. The process control limits may be seen as a matter of local, process-management interest. If data points show up that are outside of the process control band or if some trend shows up within the process control band, local management will want to step in to find out what has changed in the process to cause this deviant behavior.

The system limits are a matter of interest to higher management because the interfaces between operating departments are represented by the system limits. Local initiatives to improve the process may be offered up to the organization as proposed tightening of the system limits. On the other hand, the local management can defend the present system limits on the process by producing process control charts and asserting that that is the way things are and that the system limits can only be changed if measures are taken to improve the process itself.

To take the simple example above, we will start with the chart that is based on all seven days of performance. Local management can say that the present system, which has poor performance on weekends, requires that the system limits be set at a high level, as is shown on the following control chart. The upper system limit is at 38 units, and the lower system limit is at zero. No points appear anywhere near the upper system limit. That is to be expected, for only a few points in a million would approach this limit, and with only seven daily total samples on this chart, few-in-a-million events are not likely.

Should the system limit be drawn at a lower level, thereby soaking up the white space between the process control limit and the system upper limit? That can only be done at the risk that data points will impinge on the system limit just through normal process fluctuation much more often than a few times in a million. Given that the whole point of Six Sigma is to prevent that, Six Sigma policy is to leave the upper system limit alone.

FIGURE 18: CONTROL CHART WITH SYSTEM LIMITS

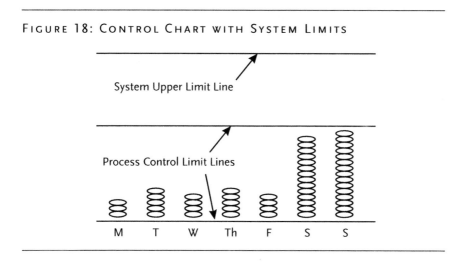

Now, the charts draw attention to the weekend data. If something were done differently on the weekends, that would constitute a *change in the process*. If the steps bring the weekend data down to about the level of the weekday points, the process control limits and the system limits can be redrawn after a suitable trial period. The contraction of the system limits could then be used as a basis to revise the interface with the neighboring operating unit and to improve overall system performance.

Data Tracking

Track the process by plotting data points as they happen on a process control chart. Set the process control limits by calculating the average value and the standard deviation of the samples in hand. If the sample count is lower than 20, redo the calculations when 20 samples are in hand. Over time, redo the calculations about once a month.

Examine the process control chart; that is the point of doing it in the first place. Are the plotted points within the control band? Are the plotted points balanced around the average? Are the plotted points showing a periodic pattern? Are the plotted points drifting away from the average?

We will now look at the tracking of data on a typical process control chart:

FIGURE 19: TYPICAL TRACKING CHART

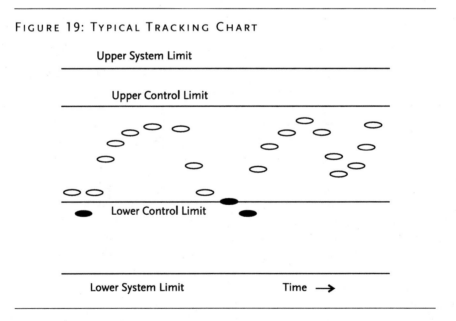

Are there exceptional points that call for further attention?

This chart shows one point right on the process control lower limit and two points below the process control lower limit (highlighted as black dots on the chart). In this case, at least two and probably three points merit special attention, and some legwork is in order to see if it can be determined what was different on those two or three occasions. It cannot be ruled out that these are just naturally occurring points from the distribution, but they look odd and should be checked out.

Now look at the rest of the points, which show a pronounced cyclical pattern. Cyclical patterns are common enough, often following day/night or early-in-shift/late-in-shift patterns. The fact that there is a cyclical pattern is not necessarily a concern, but it is something that might bear a little further study. Perhaps the process could be changed to reduce the swing over the cycle, such as by retraining or getting equipment tuned up before the shift starts. If the cyclic swing could be cut in half, the process control limit band would be cut about in half and the system limit band could be cut about in half, which would lead in general to an improvement in the overall system performance.

Note that the process control band is not centered between the system limits. This should be marked for eventual consideration, even if the present ratios meet the Six Sigma design rules.

We will now consider another tracking example:

FIGURE 20: PROCESS TRACKING WITH DRIFT

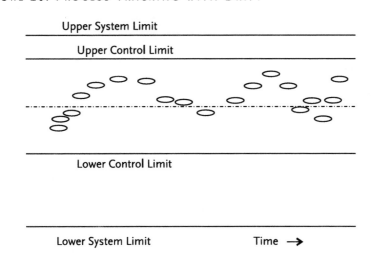

This is a similar plot to the previous figure, but note that here all of the points are within the process control band. The cyclical pattern appears again, and there now seems to be a bit of an upward drift, too. It looks like the bottom points are moving up more than the top points, so the average may be shifting upward. This hypothesis can be tested by tracking the average separately (as will be considered below), but for the time being, we will look at what this chart shows.

The process is believed to be following a normal distribution, and because the normal distribution is symmetric with regard to its average value, half of the points should be below the average line, and half should be above. What are the odds that the next point will be above the average? One in two. What are the odds that the next two points will be above the average? One in four. The next three points? One in eight. The next four points? One in 16. The next five points? One in 32. The next ten points above the line? Less than one in 1,000. So, if several points in a row (or nearly all of several points in a row) fall on one side of the average, the process has probably somehow changed and some unknown event is currently causing this to happen. Now would be a good time to look into the matter, before the process drifts so far that the system limits are in jeopardy.

Management View of Multistep Processes

The average yield of a multistep process is the product of the average yields of the individual steps. The average duration of a multistep process is the sum of the average durations of the individual steps. The standard deviations add like the sides of triangles, by taking the square root of the sum of the squares.

We now consider a four-step process with yields and durations as shown in this table.

Stage	Yield	Standard Deviation Yield	Duration	Standard Deviation Duration
			Hours	Hours
1	99%	1%	2	0.3
2	95%	2%	12	1.5
3	95%	2%	8	0.5
4	94%	4%	1	0.1
Combined	84%	5%	23	1.6

Looking at each step individually shows that the yields, although not particularly good, do not look particularly bad. Combined, they look pretty bad. If only 84 percent of patients are getting their treatment right the first time all the way through, that means that 16 percent, on average, are being held up for additional treatment or to fix paperwork or something else unplanned. On first approximation, 16 percent of the organization's effort is going toward rework.

Suppose we calculate control limits and system limits on the four-step process.

	Yield	Duration
Control Limits		
Upper	99%	27.8
Lower	69%	18.2
System Limits		
Upper	100%	32.7
Lower	54%	13.3

The control limits are approached a few times per 1,000, so the organization can expect to see as few as 69 percent of any group of patients flowing through the system with no error and, consequently, as many as 31 percent of any group of patients being held up for rework. The organization can expect to see treatment durations ranging from 18 to 28 hours.

On a conservative planning basis, management would use the system limit values, planning on a contingency basis to see yields as low as 54 percent for any group of patients and durations as high as 33 hours. Management may elect to study more closely those cases that flow through the system very quickly. There is something favorable about these. Are they a peculiar group of people? Are they being treated in some particular way that others are not? Is something here to be learned that might apply to the population as a whole?

Management can also study the least favorable of these cases to see what is going wrong. The bad cases get management attention because a clamor for attention will likely be raised by the patient group, by the department managers who are seeing their work backed up, and by employees who find themselves doing work twice. It takes more management willpower to look into the favorable cases because clamor is not likely, and yet it is in studying the favorable cases that a new lesson may be learned.

QUANTITATIVE PROCESS ANALYSIS

We will now look a little more closely at the quantitative methods that support Six Sigma analysis. Nothing in this section requires any higher mathematics training; all arithmetic will be presented on the basis that the reader has convenient access to a computer and a spreadsheet application. The specifics here will follow Microsoft Excel® nomenclature; all spreadsheets have these same functions although they may have slightly different names and arrangements of arguments.

We want to estimate the average and standard deviation of observed values. If lots of data are in hand, getting sufficient estimates of these two parameters is very easy by using the spreadsheet functions AVERAGE(. . .) and STDEV(. . .). These can be applied to prior data to characterize the process baseline, and they can be applied during a trial to characterize the effect of the changes introduced for the purposes of the trial.

In health service processes, often relatively few data are on hand, and the rate of generating new data is rather slow. Therefore, it is often necessary to consider methods that apply to sparse data sets.

When the data sets are "rich" in number, the process average value and the process standard deviation can be tracked directly, as will be shown shortly. When the data sets are sparse, indirect methods will be developed and applied.

Tracking the Process

Plotting data points directly on a process control chart, with process limit lines at plus and minus three standard deviations and with system limits at plus and minus six standard deviations, is good practice. Points that fall outside of the process control limits are points worthy of attention every time because this should happen only a few times per 1,000. Consider these as early warnings. Points that fall outside the system limit lines are a cause for alarm because this should happen only a few times per million and will likely upset operations beyond the immediate operating unit.

If a great many data points are being generated, it may be appropriate to plot just a sample of the total data set using some rule to decide which to plot and which not to plot. Getting the sampling plan right takes some thought, and this matter will be covered in detail in one of the cases. Also, if there are a lot of data, it may be helpful to aggregate the data into subsets, perhaps by department or by shift, and plot just the subset averages and subset standard deviations. This is particularly the case for the subset averages; Six Sigma makes a special allowance for drift in the average, so observing whether any drifting is taking place is helpful.

Tracking the Process Average Directly

Set the rule for dividing up the data into subsets, perhaps by shift or by department. Calculate the average value of each subset using AVERAGE(. . .). Plot the results on a tracking plot. This plot is often called an X-bar plot, because it uses the X-bar to denote the subset averages.

FIGURE 21: TRACKING CHART FOR SAMPLE AVERAGES

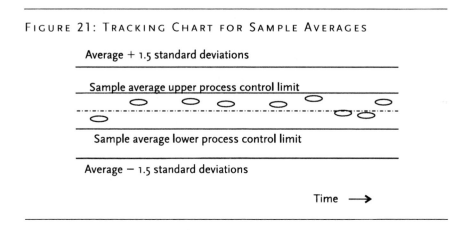

If plotted on the same scale used for plotting individual data points, the X-bar points will show a much tighter pattern than the individual data points; this is reasonable because the average will move around a lot less than individual samples.

It may be helpful to plot limit lines at 1.5 standard deviations from the established average. Six Sigma makes allowance for drift in the process average value of as much as 1.5 standard deviations. If the average shows signs of violating this allowance, it is time to pay special attention to the process to see what's going on.

It is often useful to develop process control limits for the X-bar values and to take these X-bar values as a new population. (It is a source of endless confusion that the X-bar population has its own standard deviation, which is different and distinct from the standard deviation of the underlying population. It is a good thing it does, though, because this is the basis for the central limit theorem, which will be covered in one of the cases and is the reason that the normal distribution is so popular in everyday statistical analysis.) Using the X-bar values, apply STDEV(. . .) and plot lines at plus and minus three times this value from the established process average value. If the process is well-behaved, the X-bar points will fall within these control limits except for a few times in 1,000. This is an early warning line.

The observation technique is the same. Are there exceptional points? Is there cyclic behavior? Is there drift?

Tracking the Process Standard Deviation Directly

To track the process standard deviation directly, the method is the same. First, set a rule for dividing the sample data into subsets, perhaps by shift or department. For each set, calculate the standard deviation within that set using STDEV(. . .). Plot the points; this is often called an S-plot.

If the STDEV(. . .) values are collected, they form a new population that has an average value and a standard deviation all its own. These parameters can be used to make a new control chart with limit lines at plus and minus three times the standard deviation of this new population. If points on this control chart approach these limit lines more than a few times per 1,000, it is time to pay attention. These are early warning lines.

Student

Modern applied statistics began in 1908 with the publication of "Probable Error of the Mean" by William Sealy Gosset, who was using the *nom de plume* "Student" (Student 1908). Gosset was a British brewer and an amateur mathematician.

Dealing with Sparse Data Sets

If the number of samples in the total available population is lower than about 20, the AVERAGE(. . .) and STDEV(. . .) functions will produce results, but these results are uncertain. The same is true for any subset with fewer than about 20 samples.

Some methods for dealing with these sparse data sets do not eliminate the uncertainty (that would be impossible), but they do have the merit that they tell you what that uncertainty is. These methods generate *confidence intervals*, which are bands within which the underlying population's average value and, separately, the underlying population's standard deviation are likely to fall for a given confidence level. The confidence level is stipulated by the analyst; it is typically 75 or 90 percent, occasionally 95 or 99 percent, or, sometimes just for fun, 99.9 percent.

Before getting into the arithmetic, let us do the following mental exercise. Suppose there are 25 people in a room, and their average age is calculated down to the day. For this example, this age will be 27 years and 87 days. Now, if we take a sample of five people from that same group and calculate their average age, would we expect to get 27 years and 87 days? No; we would expect to get some other average for this small subgroup. Suppose we increase the sample size to ten people and calculate the average age of this group. We would not expect to get 27 years and 87 days, but we could expect to get closer to that because the sample is larger. Suppose we took a sample of 20. Intuitively we would expect to be getting a very good estimate of the real average number.

Now, rather than expecting to get the right answer, suppose we ask only that we get *close to* the right answer. Suppose we ask that we get within 30 days of the right answer, or 60 days, or 90 days. If some cost is involved in getting each value, we might do a tradeoff between cost and precision of result; this would also cause us to consider just how much precision we really need in the answer.

Suppose we now say that we want to know how confident we can be that the answer is really within our stipulated range of, say, 30 days. Can we be 100 percent confident? 95 percent confident? 75 percent confident? 50 percent confident? If we are betting that the right answer is within the specified range, what odds do we want to take that the right answer is within this range?

When we deal with sparse data, we make estimates of the average value and standard deviation, and these estimates are intervals. We combine a confidence level and a sample size, and we compute the interval. The higher the confidence level we set, the wider the interval; the smaller the sample size, the wider the interval. A wide interval may be worthless to us, so we set about gathering more data to increase the sample size and thereby reduce the interval size.

A high degree of confidence in the outcome is not always needed, and in these cases a lower confidence level can be used and a smaller interval computed. We will be wrong more often, but we will know that when we set the confidence level.

Two statistical methods will be applied when using the Six Sigma process. For the confidence interval for the population average value, the *Student's t* method and distribution are applied. For confidence intervals for the population standard deviation, the *chi-square* (the sound is hard, as in "chiropractor") method and distribution will be applied.

These methods are easy enough to apply if a spreadsheet is available to do the arithmetic. The method will be shown below, and tables of results covering the usual range of interest will be provided as well. If you are doing analysis with a spreadsheet, you can follow the method given here. If you are doing analysis by hand, just use the tabulated results below.

If these methods are applied to rich populations (those with a lot of sample values), they will give a confidence interval that is only a little larger than a point; they do not provide any useful information if there is hardly any uncertainty in the calculations. Therefore, for rich populations, confidence intervals are not worth the bother.

Confidence Intervals for the Population Average Value

Proceed as follows:

1. Select the sample set to be analyzed and note the number of samples.
2. Compute the set average and standard deviation using AVERAGE(. . .) and STDEV(. . .).
3. Select a confidence level such as 90 percent.
4. Compute the inverse Student-t factor by TINV(100 percent minus the confidence level, number of samples). For example, you would enter TINV(100% − 90%, 15) for a confidence level of 90 percent and a sample size of 15. Call the result t'.
5. Multiply the STDEV(. . .) value by t'. Add this to the AVERAGE(. . .) result to get the upper limit on the confidence interval and subtract the same from the AVERAGE(. . .) value to get the lower limit on the confidence interval.
6. If this is being applied to subsets, plotting the intervals can be instructive.

Here is a quick example:

Calculating Confidence Intervals for the Average: Spreadsheet Method	
Count	15
Confidence level	90%
TINV(100% − confidence level, number of samples)	1.753
Sample average value	12.7
Sample standard deviation	1.8
Confidence interval, upper limit	15.86
Confidence interval, lower limit	9.54

The meaning of *confidence interval* is this: the likelihood that the true value lies within this interval is equal to the asserted confidence level. So, if the asserted confidence level is 90 percent, the likelihood is 90 percent that the confidence interval covers the true value. The converse is also true: if the confidence level is 90 percent, there is a 10 percent chance that the true value is *not* covered by the interval. If this is done repeatedly over time, the confidence intervals will be seen to cover the true value about as often as would be expected from the confidence level asserted.

Consider the following chart, which shows 20 confidence intervals computed in this way for a 75 percent confidence level and sample sizes of ten. These are all drawn from a normal distribution having average value of zero. One would expect that about three-quarters of the confidence intervals would cover the zero line. Fifteen of them do, and two others come close, so this is about as expected. Even so, three of the intervals seem to be quite far away from the zero line, and if it were the analyst's bad luck to draw these, the analyst could be led astray.

FIGURE 22: TRACKING CHART FOR CONFIDENCE INTERVALS ON THE AVERAGE VALUE

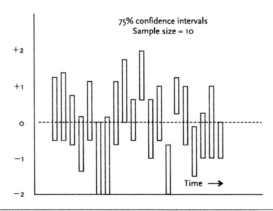

As more data come to hand, the uncertainty can be reduced by including the additional data points in the analysis. If all 200 of the points used to plot these confidence intervals were used to calculate the average, the result is a confidence interval of 0.08, which is pretty close to zero. This shows that using sparse-data analysis, including confidence intervals, while a larger data set is being gathered, can be useful. Even with the inherent uncertainty, some information, properly interpreted, is better than none.

Here is a table showing the multipliers to use in calculating the confidence intervals on the average value for a range commonly of interest. Select an entry from the table, multiply the selected entry times the sample standard deviation found by STDEV(. . .), then add the product to (subtract the product from) the sample average value found by AVERAGE(. . .) to get the upper (lower) confidence interval limit on the average value of the underlying population.

Multipliers for Average Value Confidence Intervals

Count	50% Confidence	75% Confidence	90% Confidence
5	0.727	1.301	2.015
10	0.700	1.221	1.812
15	0.691	1.197	1.753
20	0.687	1.185	1.725

To do the same example from above, using the table instead of the spreadsheet formula, you would proceed as follows:

Calculating Confidence Intervals for the Average: Tabulated Values Method

Count	15
Confidence level	90%
T value from table for this count and confidence level	1.753
Sample average value	12.7
Sample standard deviation	1.8
Confidence interval, upper limit	15.86
Confidence interval, lower limit	9.54

Confidence Intervals for the Population Standard Deviation

The logic for using confidence intervals rather than point values is the same for the population standard deviation as it is for the population average value. If the data set is sparse, using a confidence interval gets better results than believing the point value provided by STDEV(. . .). Indeed, using confidence intervals for the standard deviation is even more appropriate because the standard deviation settles down more slowly as the sample count increases than the average value does. The mechanics for both, however, are nearly the same. The chi-square method and distribution are used to compute the confidence interval for the standard deviation. The steps are as follows:

1. Note the sample set size, say 15.
2. Select a confidence level, say 75 percent. Select two limits, the difference between which equals the confidence level, say 87.5 percent and 12.5 percent.
3. For each of these, compute the chi-square factor by applying CHIINV (upper limit, set count less one), for our example, CHIINV(87.5%, 14). Repeat for the lower limit, CHIINV(12.5%, 14).
4. Calculate the upper multiplier by taking the square root of the ratio of (sample count less one) over the upper chi-square factor from step 3, in this case, SQRT[14/CHIINV(87.5%, 14)]. Repeat using the lower limit to get the lower multiplier, in this case, SQRT[14/CHIINV(12.5%, 14)].
5. Compute the set standard deviation with STDEV(. . .).
6. Multiply the set standard deviation by the upper multiplier to get the upper end of the confidence interval. Repeat using the lower multiplier to get the lower end of the confidence interval. Doing this all at once, the upper limit would be, for this example, STDEV(. . .) * SQRT[14/CHIINV(14, 87.5%)], and the lower limit would be, for this example, STDEV(. . .) * SQRT[14/CHIINV(4, 12.5%)].

Note that the set average value plays no part in the calculation of the confidence interval for the standard deviation.

Here is an example worked out:

Calculating Confidence Intervals for the Standard Deviation: Spreadsheet Method

Count	15
Confidence level	75%
Upper cutoff	87.5%
Lower cutoff	12.5%

(continued)

Chi-square factor, upper	8.266
Chi-square factor, lower	20.166
Upper multiplier	1.301
Lower multiplier	0.833
Sample standard deviation, taken from example above	1.8
Upper confidence interval limit on standard deviation	2.343
Lower confidence interval limit on standard deviation	1.500

This arithmetic is easy enough for a spreadsheet to do, but it is exactly the sort of step-by-step arithmetic that invites trouble when done by hand. To keep the by-hand analyst out of trouble, the following table skips all of the arithmetic and just gives the multipliers to be applied to the sample standard deviation for a useful range of confidence levels and sample sizes.

Multipliers to Apply to the Sample Standard Deviation

Sample	50% Confidence		75% Confidence		90% Confidence	
Count	Lower	Upper	Lower	Upper	Lower	Upper
5	0.862	1.442	0.745	1.812	0.649	2.372
10	0.889	1.235	0.804	1.413	0.729	1.645
15	0.904	1.174	0.833	1.301	0.769	1.460
20	0.915	1.142	0.852	1.246	0.794	1.370

These multipliers get applied to the sample standard deviation to get the upper and lower limits on the confidence interval for the population's standard deviation.

Here is the same example, worked from the table:

Calculating Confidence Intervals for the Standard Deviation: Tabulated Values Method

Count	15
Confidence level	75%
Upper multiplier from table	1.301
Lower multiplier from table	0.833
Sample standard deviation, taken from example above	1.8
Upper confidence interval limit on standard deviation	2.343
Lower confidence interval limit on standard deviation	1.500

Note that the upper and lower multipliers are not equal; this is because the chi-square distribution is not symmetric.

Here is a chart of some confidence intervals on the population standard deviation with various confidence level requirements and sample sizes. The samples are drawn from a normal distribution with standard deviation equal to unity.

FIGURE 23: EFFECT OF SAMPLE COUNT ON STANDARD DEVIATION CONFIDENCE INTERVAL SIZE

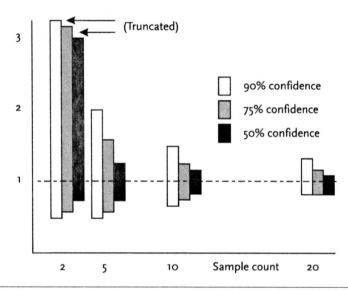

For the sample count of two, the 90 percent and 75 percent confidence bars are truncated at the upper end to keep them in the chart. The actual numbers are about 15 and 6, which means that the bars are so long as to be worthless for estimating where the underlying standard deviation might be.

Each of the bars represents a confidence interval, and the longer the bar, the less helpful the estimate. To put it more positively, a smaller bar gives a more helpful estimate.

A 50 percent confidence factor is the lowest confidence factor worth the bother. A 75 percent confidence factor is reasonable for general tracking of sample data, and a confidence factor of 90 or 95 percent should be held for those applications where there are plenty of sample points and the significance of the result is great.

To confirm that the behavior of confidence intervals on the population's standard deviation follows the behavior of confidence intervals on the population's average value, here is a chart showing 20 different confidence intervals computed by taking samples from the same normal distribution having a true standard deviation of 2.00.

FIGURE 24: TRACKING CHART FOR CONFIDENCE INTERVALS ON THE STANDARD DEVIATION

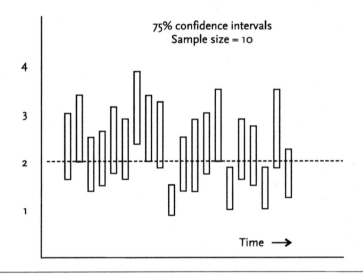

Because the asserted confidence level is 75 percent, one would expect about three-quarters of the confidence intervals to cover the true value, which is the 2.00 line. Four of the confidence intervals do not cover the 2.00 line, and a couple of the others appear to just touch it; that would seem to be consistent with a 75 percent confidence interval, by definition, because about three-quarters of the intervals cover the known and true standard deviation

With all 200 data points in hand (using all 20 of the sets of ten samples), applying STDEV(. . .) returns a point estimate for the population's standard deviation of 1.996. Compare that with the true value of 2.00. Once again, having plenty of data points reduces uncertainty and allows the analyst to skip the bother of calculating confidence intervals.

The application of the confidence interval to the population standard deviation for sparse data sets is this: use the confidence interval cautiously until more data points come to light. Having an estimate, even with uncertainty, is better than having no information at all. Using STDEV(. . .) to do a point estimate of the population standard deviation with a sparse data set is rash.

Repeatability and Reproducibility

Employee teams repeat tasks. The extent to which the outcomes are about the same, time after time, is called *repeatability*. Different employee teams also do these same tasks. The extent to which the second group has outcomes that are about the same as those of the first group is called *reproducibility*. Repeatability and reproducibility are interesting to isolate because different actions are required to improve each.

This analysis is traditionally called *gauge analysis* because the original question was, "How variable are worker A's readings of a certain gauge, and how much difference does it make if worker B reads the gauge instead?" With digital gauges these days, that issue has largely gone away. However, for other tasks, the issue is still germane. For instance, it may be of interest to compare the results of work done on different shifts, work done by novices versus that done by experienced staff, winter versus summer, hot day versus cold day, or any other discriminating parameter.

Suppose data are available for the outcomes of a task, and suppose it is known which tasks were done by group A and which were done by group B. We wish to know if any significant difference is found between the two groups.

Proceed as follows:

Calculate the average values and standard deviations for subset A and subset B using AVERAGE(. . .) and STDEV(. . .). If they look to be about the same, operate on the basis that they *are* the same (that no distinction exists between group A and group B), at least until more data come to hand.

If they look to be somewhat different, take guidance from the following table:

Sample Count	Difference	Action
~100 or more	Large	Believe the values
	Small	Believe the values
~50 or so	Large	Believe the direction
	Small	Believe no change

(continued on following page)

(Continued)

~25 or so	Large	Do confidence test
	Small	Believe no change
~10 or so	Large	Get more data
	Small	Get more data

The confidence tests, which will now be described, can be applied to any sample size. However, for large sample sizes, the result will just confirm what direct observation has already told you, and for tiny sample sizes, the result will not give you much guidance. For middle-size samples, doing some simple analysis is worthwhile if only to help decide whether to try to get more data so that more precision can be obtained in the analysis.

Step 1. Are the average values different? Use the following test to see if the underlying populations have the same average value.

Tabulate the sample subsets in a spreadsheet.

Apply built-in function TTEST(first sample set, second sample set); TTEST is the Excel® function that uses the Student's t function to calculate the probabilities. The value returned by TTEST is a probability that the means of the two underlying populations are the same, in this case, say 67 percent.

This test is certainly easy to do, but it is very sensitive to small changes in the sample data. Such changes, which may be hardly noticeable to the analyst, might cause the result to change from 66 to 50 percent, so caution is in order. To see the sensitivity, consider four sets of 25 data points all drawn from the same underlying population. Because the underlying population is the same, the "right answer" is a high confidence that each pair are the same. The question at hand is, does the TTEST analysis give the high-confidence answer?

Set Pairs	Confidence Factor that the Sets Save the Same Average Value
A-B	95%
A-C	81%
A-D	97%
B-C	74%
B-D	99%
C-D	76%

Some of these pairs show high confidence that they have the same mean, but for one pair, B-C, the confidence level is rather modest at 74 percent, and for another pair, C-D, the confidence level is only slightly better at 76 percent. In the normal course of events, the analyst would not have four sets but only two, and knowing that the results may depend on chance, the analyst will proceed with some caution.

The next question is what to do with the answer. If the answer is 93 percent, the test may be helpful because it would reveal that the two populations very likely have the same average value. If the answer is 4 percent, the test may be helpful because it is saying that the two populations very likely do *not* have the same average value. If the answer is 43, 55, or 68 percent, you're stuck. More data are needed.

Step 2. Are the standard deviations different? Tabulate the sample subsets in a spreadsheet.

Apply built-in function FTEST(first sample set, second sample set). FTEST is the Excel® function using the F distribution to calculate the probabilities. The function returns, say, 45 percent.

This test is also easy to do, and, like the TTEST, it is very sensitive to small changes in the data sets and must be used cautiously. More data will always help. If the outcome is neither near one nor near zero, the test is inconclusive and more data are required.

Here is the FTEST applied to the same four sets of 25 samples each, all drawn from the same normal distribution.

Set Pairs	Confidence that the Sets Have the Same Standard Deviation
A-B	13%
A-C	78%
A-D	37%
B-C	21%
B-D	52%
C-D	54%

This table uses exactly the same data sets as were used above to test for same/different average values. This time, the test is to find the same/different standard deviations. The answers are much worse, being neither very close to unity nor close to zero. In fact, the answers are no help at all.

This is often the case when testing for the standard deviation with modest-sized samples because the standard deviation is much more volatile than the average value. The only cure is to get more data. Suspend judgment in the meantime.

Analysis of Variance: Regression

The *variance* of a distribution is the square of the standard deviation. It happens that variances can be added together and subtracted from one another. If there are only two variables, say length and weight, the variance of the entire set can be decomposed into a variance with length, a variance with weight, and perhaps a cross-term varying with both length and weight. Because of this, it is useful to apply this law to gain insight into the workings of the process being examined.

One common application is called *regression,* which is the fitting of a formula to fit the data set. The most common formula to fit is that of a straight line. Excel® and other spreadsheets do the heavy lifting, so a few keystrokes will provide an analysis. Rather than derive formulas here, we will proceed to look at examples.

FIGURE 25: LINEAR REGRESSION EXAMPLE

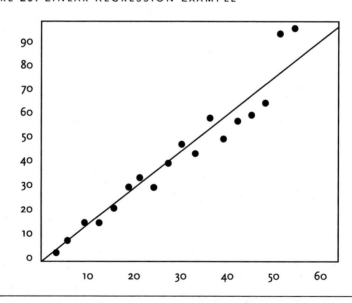

In the first case, a straight line is fitted to a collection of points that look like a straight line using the Excel® linear regression tool. The chart above shows that this might be a reasonable model; this is known because we asked the spreadsheet to plot both the data and the fitted line so that the goodness of fit can be inspected by eye. This is always good practice in statistical analysis because, although the computer can do the arithmetic, the analyst has to provide the common sense. In this case, the fit appears to be reasonable, but it is not very good at the right-hand end of the data.

Excel® not only gives the fitted parameters, it gives a lot of analysis of its work. However, the Excel® labeling is obscure, so several of the Excel® labels and their hidden meaning will be supplied here.

Excel® Label	Meaning
ANOVA	Analysis of variance
Degrees of freedom	Degrees of freedom
SS	Sum of squares
MS	Mean of the sum of squares
F	Value from the F distribution
Significance	Goodness of fit value
Regression	Variability accounted for by the fit
Residual	Variability remaining after the fit
Intercept	Y value when X = 0
X variable 1	Slope of the fitted line

Excel® does use additional labels and values, but we will not get into them here.

The degrees of freedom are related to the size of the sample set. The total number of degrees of freedom is equal to the size of the sample set. One degree of freedom is assigned in the analysis to the fit, and the rest of the degrees of freedom are assigned to the residual, which is to say the lack of fit, point by point.

The F value is from the F distribution, and a higher value is better than a lower value. Whether the F value is high enough can be evaluated by looking at the significance value computed by Excel®. In this case, a low number is good. A significance value *below* the level of interest, say 5 percent, means that the fit is good "at the 5 percent level of significance." The significance level is the complement of the confidence level; a significance level of 5 percent corresponds to a confidence level of 95 percent.

Another way of determining the goodness of fit is to look at the sum of squares (SS) value for the regression as a proportion of the total sum of squares. If the proportion is high, the fit is better than if the proportion is low. There is no numerical test for good versus bad for this parameter.

The Excel® regression analysis is not a function; rather, it is a tool. To find it, select the tools menu, then select data analysis, then select regression. (If the tools menu does not show a data analysis item in the list, you must make Excel® install it. To do this, from the menu select tools, then add-ins, and then check analysis toolpak. Close the window, then go again to the tools menu, and the data analysis entry will appear in the tools list.) Follow the instructions to select the dependent and independent variables you have elected, and tell Excel® where to exhibit the results.

Caution: Excel® does not reapply this tool if the data change. So, if the data change, it is necessary to repeat the steps above to force Excel® to repeat the regression analysis. Excel® does not warn you about this, so be careful.

Here are the data points used to give the regression line in the chart above:

X	Y	X	Y
2	3.57	22	27.86
4	6.23	24	42.38
6	11.97	26	33.89
8	8.27	28	51.09
10	15.02	30	37.1
12	21.97	32	39.71
14	26.02	34	46.21
16	17.03	36	46.23
18	25.58	38	51.9
20	33.44	40	78.74

Regression Analysis: Straight Line Fit

Result	Value
Intercept	0.23
Confidence interval on intercept, lower end	−6.63
Confidence interval on intercept, upper end	7.09

(continued on following page)

X variable 1 (slope)	1.48
Confidence interval on slope, lower end	1.19
Confidence interval on slope, upper end	1.76

The confidence intervals are calculated at a 95 percent confidence level by default.

Let us now look at the results. The confidence interval on the intercept is −6.63 to +7.09. This is a pretty wide confidence interval, so we cannot have much confidence that we know the intercept very well at all. The confidence interval for the slope is 1.19 to 1.76. This is also a little on the wide side. Both fitted parameters are only somewhat pinned down.

Look again at the fitted line and the data points in the chart above. By inspection, the fit is pretty good. Yet, as we just saw by analysis, the fit is rather uncertain; this shows that the analytic tools are awfully conservative by their very nature. However, that is the best analysis anybody knows how to do, so it is up to the analyst to consider matters and make a judgment. Using the calculated values blindly is not good practice.

As another example, consider a regression analysis of another set of data, this one showing a cyclic pattern.

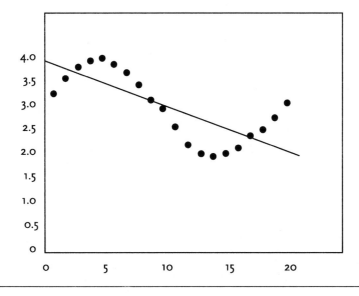

FIGURE 26: LINEAR REGRESSION ON CYCLICAL DATA

Here, the Excel® regression tool has fitted a straight line, and the fitted line seems to balance points above against points below the line. However, the fit does not make any sense because a straight line is a very poor model for the data. (Hint: That is the point of this example.)

Let us see if Excel® tells us that the fit does not make any sense:

Result	Value
Intercept	3.96
Confidence interval on intercept, lower end	3.48
Confidence interval on intercept, upper end	4.44
X variable 1 (slope)	−0.09
Confidence interval on slope, lower end	−0.13
Confidence interval on slope, upper end	−0.05

In this case, the confidence intervals are quite narrow. The confidence interval for the intercept is a mere 3.48 to 4.44, and the confidence interval for the slope is −0.13 to −0.05. Because both intervals are narrow, just looking at the numbers would cause the analyst to think that this straight line is a pretty good data model. However, it is not. The starting assumption, that the data can be represented by a straight line, is weak.

As with any statistical analysis, if the data sets were larger, the confidence intervals would be tighter. However, as has just been shown and can be plainly seen by looking at the fitted curve and the sample data, there is more to getting a decent fit than getting tight confidence intervals. Excel® is perfectly happy to do more complicated regressions involving more variables; the difficulty is finding some way to plot the data and the results so that some judgment can be made about the sensibility of the fitted functions. Proceed with caution. Some particular applications of multiple regression will appear later in this book.

Commercial statistical software packages include surface plotting tools that can sometimes provide a sufficient means for making a visual examination. For regression analysis going beyond one or two variables, look for a commercial package if only to get the surface plotting functionality.

To summarize:

1. To seek a relationship between variables, a regression analysis may help. Plotting the data and plotting the fitted line is absolutely necessary as part of the evaluation of the fit.

2. Visual examination of the fit is likely to be more useful than careful scrutiny of the confidence intervals or residuals or other derived statistical factors.

Time-Weighted Values

Statistics software packages usually offer to plot time-weighted values. However, these are not likely to be of interest in healthcare. The idea can be explained quickly enough. Start with the last several points, multiply the most recent value by one, the preceding value by a weighting factor, the value before that by the weighting factor squared, and so on. Add these up to get a weighted value, divide by the number of values used, and plot the result. Sometimes a more complicated divisor is used, but the idea is the same. If the weighting factor is unity, this just gives usual average of the last several data points. This is called the "boxcar average."

If the weighting factor is less than 1, say 0.8, the more distant points are multiplied by smaller and smaller factors and contribute less and less to the final weighted value. This puts emphasis on the last point or two, and it emphasizes any lack of precision in the measurement. Because many of the data points in healthcare will be estimated and hand-recorded, they will be imprecise; therefore, emphasizing imprecise values is not likely to be helpful.

If the weighting factor is greater than 1, say 1.2, the more distant points are multiplied by greater and greater factors and contribute more and more to the final weighted value. This puts emphasis on the older points, which again may be imprecise for the same reason as above. So, weighting factors that are greater than 1 do not help much in the healthcare case, either.

Boxcar averaging might be useful in some cases, but it is not very different from the subset sampling discussed previously; it just lumps together some of the data subsets. In short, time-weighting is fine for some other applications, but it is not likely to be helpful in healthcare because of the imprecise data being handled. If you wish to confirm or disprove this, Excel® provides time-weighting functionality, and you can experiment.

Summing Up Quantitative Analysis

Tracking data is fundamental to Six Sigma problem detection. The tracked data are average values and standard deviations using data from processes of interest. When the data sets are sparse, looking at confidence intervals is the better practice. When the data sets are rich, then straightforward application of spreadsheet functions AVERAGE(. . .) and STDEV(. . .) are quite good for your purposes.

Regression analysis can sometimes bring out the influence of parameters such as work-shift effects, winter-summer effects, or the like. All data and analysis are to be used cautiously because the starting data are likely to be imprecise. More data always help.

Change Management

Improving the system will require changes to be made. However, the changes are first to be tried out on some small scale so that lessons can be learned without risking the whole of the organization.

SELECTING CHANGES

The first thing to be decided when making changes is whether you want to make many small ones or a few big ones. The following pages will address some of the positive and negative aspects of both routes.

Many Small Changes

Deming favored participation by everybody on the basis of the idea that the worker is the important element and that letting the worker improve processes is key. This is the "hurdle" notion: workers would be more successful if hurdles were removed, and who knows better what the hurdles are than the actual worker? A small group of workers or the small team of workers from various departments will know and identify the hurdles.

Quality Circles

In the 1980s, many American firms experimented with *quality circles,* an idea imported from Japan. A quality circle is a group of employees— not managers—drawn from adjacent departments who select a small improvement to be made. They make this improvement by drawing small amounts of money from the organization as might be needed to carry it out. These quality circles seemed to do some good and very little harm, and they were an interesting experiment in industrial group dynamics. However, American interest in them seems to have waned in recent years. The improvements were almost guaranteed to work because those involved in making them work were the very same people who sponsored the improvement.

Quality circles were generally operated on lunch breaks and were "unmanaged," so the cost to the organization was small. In Japan, quality circles commonly meet in the evening, on noncompany time. Quality circles are one way of getting to Deming's ideal, but other ways are available.

Campaigns

A campaign is another way of getting lots of smaller things done. In a campaign, one particular goal is set, and everybody is encouraged to meet it by the end of the month or day. Crosby favors "zero defect day" campaigns. Wal-Mart features pep rallies for its associates who work on the store floor. These are one-day-at-a-time campaigns. Although many people find such campaigns annoying, distracting, unprofessional, and not at all motivating, the fact is that some people respond to campaigns very positively. Varsity athletes are given pep talks and immediate goals to reach (win the game, score the goal, hit the ball). Because these athletes have been hearing the same pep talks since they were eight years old, they are conditioned to respond with increased concentration and effort. Sales departments run on campaigns, with those who meet the special monthly sales goal winning a steak dinner or a trip to Hawaii. All sales departments run campaigns, and all salespeople are motivated to concentrate all the harder to meet their goals; it is therefore not surprising to find that many companies go out of their way to hire varsity athletes to work in their sales departments.

Suggestion Boxes

Mandatory suggestion boxes are a different sort of campaign, with the same campaign being repeated again and again. Employees are exhorted to turn in suggestions for improvement of the workplace or the products. Because they are exhorted, they feel some pressure to think up something to suggest; this gets the employees' heads involved in the game at least for a long enough time to think of some new idea. Some Japanese companies, with very gentle exhortation, get hundreds of suggestions per month *per employee*. The likelihood that any of these will be red-hot suggestions is small, but if the purpose is to keep the employee thinking about the job, mandatory suggestion plans will likely meet that goal. On the other hand, a passive suggestion box, lacking the exhortation, is likely to occupy the mind of few employees.

Whether active or passive, suggestion boxes take up some management time and therefore have a cost because somebody has to read the suggestions and may be expected to prepare a response to the originator. Japanese companies seem to like their mandatory suggestion box system. American and European firms that are pleased with their passive suggestion boxes seem to be few.

Few, Larger Changes

Juran (1995) favors undertaking fewer, larger changes. In fact, Juran goes so far as to say that only those changes that pose a breakthrough potential (something of great commercial value) should be undertaken at all. This is an extreme position, but extreme positions can help clarify thinking.

The fact that management is already busy argues in favor of doing few changes at a time. Any significant project will require management attention. Any project crossing organizational lines will take more management attention, and significant projects will likely cross organizational lines in a healthcare organization because of the way the work flows through the organization. Nontrivial projects require funding for capital equipment and expenses, even at the trial stage. This necessarily involves management.

Changes almost always have unforeseen ripple effects. These ripple effects may be positive or negative; one hopes for the positive. In either case, the ripples have to be looked after and understood. Gaining this understanding is not likely if several projects are causing ripples at the same time.

Other things are also going on in the organization that must be taken into consideration, with new equipment being acquired to replace old, facilities being renovated, managers being promoted, new treatments being added to the repertoire, new regulations being promulgated by various agencies, and new people being added to respond to turnover and growth. These all demand management attention as well as resources, and management can only do so much.

The Choice of Many versus Few

The many-versus-few choice is up to the organization's senior management. We personally recommend fewer projects, as we find the Juran argument persuasive on balance and solicitous of the management burden.

If the choice is made to go with a few projects, how will you know which ones are most necessary? Experience shows that the senior management knows where the problems are because they hear about them all the time. The senior group may not know what the problem is exactly, and it is not at all likely to have useful quantitative information in hand. However, they know where the problems are because everybody tells them. The senior management group could make a pretty good list of projects just by polling their own group. Indeed, Juran recommends exactly this. This process gets right to the point.

Management may choose to invite mid-level management to participate in project targeting, or it may invite a cross-section of management and professional staff. This decision is a question of local management style, and there is merit in maintaining consistency in this arena.

Thinking through the Proposal

One of the formulations of Murphy's Law is that nature sides with the hidden flaw. Thinking through any proposed trial change includes thinking about the things that can go wrong by drawing on experience, the knowledge of the staff and the institution, and knowledge of the particular change. This is known as potential problem analysis.

The point of this type of analysis is to anticipate the ripple effects that the candidate change may cause and to determine if the change should be modified or extended in some way to head off the ripples. Consider the following chart, which has to do with things that might go wrong with a mail cart that has a new wheel design. What potential problems come with a new wheel design? Some possibilities are that the new wheel design may not work or that the wheel might come off or break.

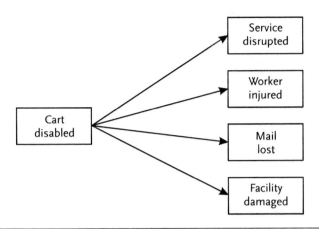

The chart helps focus attention on what problems might arise and helps with the thinking through of any mitigating actions that ought to be planned in or modifications to the proposed change that should be made. The chart may bring out some particular matters that ought to be tested specifically during the trial period.

Potential problem analysis is simple enough in practice and is generally found to be worthwhile if kept to a suitable level of detail/nondetail.

The Nature of Trials

If management had had all the quantitative information in hand in an organized way with clear implications identified, it would have made the change a long time ago. The likely starting point, then, is a general notion of what to do and where to do it but without a quantified basis for making the decision. Therefore, the way to proceed is to quantify the baseline, design a change, try it out in a small way, look hard at the outcome, quantify the results, and decide whether to extend the change to the whole organization. The trial may be localized to one group doing one activity, but it is more likely to be a trial along one workflow set of activities.

Gathering information to characterize the existing system is necessarily the first step so that the results of the trial can be compared with something in a quantitative way. Once the existing system is suitably characterized, the trial can be designed with specific goals written down.

The trial is then carried out, and both the data anticipated in the trial design and the unexpected data (ripples), which caused management, in its wisdom, to test the change in trial size in the first place, are gathered.

With the trial data in hand, a reasoned recommendation can be made to accept or reject the change. Except in trivial cases, some uncertainty will surround that recommendation. Analysis can quantify this, but it cannot eliminate it. The final decision to accept or reject the change rests with management.

The Participants Decide the Outcome

Most people are happy to participate in a trial. They figure it might be fun, and it if works they can brag about their participation later. If it fails, they will at least have stories to tell on bowling night. These folks can be counted on to give it a try, figure out little adjustments to make the change work better, and give straight feedback to the project leader.

However, those who are threatened by the trial are unlikely to be helpful in carrying it out, no matter how remote the threat. How threatened people feel has very little to do with what is said to them when the trial starts and much more to do with how the organization has behaved in comparable situations in times past. If the organization has a sorry track record in this regard, that is hard to overcome in one trial or even ten.

People can also be expected to be hostile toward the trial if it is perceived as an evaluation of *them* rather than of the work or workflow. To the extent that the trial shows that some people are making errors and the trial highlights those errors, it may well be concluded that the trial is a test of the workers themselves. What to do?

The answer is to make sure that the trial is interpreted as a test of the *system* and not of the *people*. If a person is doing a task incorrectly, that is not a failing of the person, it is a failing of the system that did not teach that person how to do the task.

However, how does the system treat people who are not correctly trained? Does the supervisor chastise the worker with a birch switch? Does the supervisor ask the worker if retraining is in order or if the task setup is wrong? Does the supervisor post control charts or their equivalent without names and let workers ask for retraining? Does retraining put the person's job at risk? Do workers even know if they are doing the task correctly? Does the system punish mistakes, thereby encouraging them to be hidden?

Encouraging Mistakes?

At this writing, a very large bank is trying to find $800,000,000 in federal income tax payment checks. The bank was under contract to the IRS to process tax payments. The contract gave no bonus to the bank for doing good work, but the contract applied a penalty for every error. So the errors disappeared, as did the checks.

It is easy to say, and Deming says it, that the workers must believe that the issue is always with the system, not with themselves. Furthermore, the workers must believe that management believes it. Deming goes further, saying that workers should never be given performance appraisals because they are given based on the notion that the person can do something to improve his or her own performance, which Deming believes goes against the "it-is-the-system-that-is-deficient" model.

Whether many organizations get to the Deming state is not known and seems unlikely. However, in the healthcare field, much of the service rests with professionals who are self-motivated in the first place and may come reasonably close to being Deming's model employees. These professionals set the tone for the whole organization. If the professionals are supportive of trials and of change, the organization has a reasonable shot at getting fair results from any trial.

Whether or not performance appraisals are used, management must review its evaluation process for *supervisors* to make sure that nothing in the trial is antithetical to the interests of the supervisors of the work activity. If a supervisor is being evaluated and rewarded on the basis of moving patients through an activity as fast as possible and if the trial holds patients up to prevent overloading the next location, something has to give. All such incentives/disincentives need to be considered in the design of any change to the system; potential problem analysis applies.

With that in mind, the trial is run in the obvious way:

1. Send out a draft to get comments beforehand.
2. Walk everybody through it.
3. Train anybody who needs training.
4. Track the data, share the data, post the data.
5. Watch for exceptions, hidden defects in the plan, and employee response. Walk around and listen to people.
6. Do not jump to premature conclusions. Get enough data and take enough time.
7. Be dispassionate.
8. Be ready to kill the trial if things do not work out.
9. Take notes. This education is expensive.

In-Trial Data Gathering

The trial will have specific objectives that can be quantified beforehand. Any one activity will have only two characteristic parameters: the average

Numbers

Numbers are important, but they are not everything. Collecting anecdotes, feelings, and impressions is important, too.

value and the standard deviation. The trial intends to move one of these, or perhaps both, but that is all it can hope to do.

Data gathering proceeds as follows:

1. The baseline control charts are in hand.
2. New control charts will be provided at the start of the trial showing where the data points are expected to fall.
3. Data are gathered and logged on the new control charts.
4. Exceptions, trends, and general behavior are examined throughout the trial.
5. Anecdotal information is logged as well; not everything can be reduced to numbers.
6. Decision points (off-ramps) are planned into the trial schedule. The trial leader reports to management at each of these times with a recommendation to proceed or to kill the trial.

The Bathtub Curve

The bathtub curve looks like a bathtub: high on one end, low in the middle, and high on the other end. The bathtub curve is a good representation of what very often happens in a trial, whether the trial involves machinery, people, or both.

Machinery lifetime follows the bathtub curve. Infant mortalities occur, and computer equipment is particularly prone to infant mortality. Then a long period transpires during which everything works fine, and finally, failures happen again when machines start wearing out. Curiously, people show the same sort of curve. At the beginning, mistakes are made while people are getting the hang of the new procedure. Then a long period passes when the skills are being applied with little conscious effort, and then there is a period of increasing error, when bad habits creep in.

Because these are such common characteristics, any trial can be expected to show them. As the trial begins, productivity and service may be worse than before while people and equipment get adapted to the new scheme. Too-early evaluation of the trial may give a false-negative outcome. Evaluation during the period when work is going smoothly may give a false-positive outcome. Then in the final period, workers are getting a little sloppy, and evaluation at this period may give a false-negative outcome. When is it *safe* to evaluate the trial? It is never entirely safe, because there will always be some risk of reading the results incorrectly. On the basis of the numbers, however, this can be quantified into a level of confidence that the right interpretation is being made. On the basis of the management of people, some judgment is required.

To complete the bathtub analogy, the third phase, when errors are on the upswing, invites replacement of worn hardware and retraining of people. The most conservative trials run well into this third phase so that machine maintenance and retraining can be evaluated as part of the trial. However, this is too conservative for most organizations.

FIGURE 28: BATHTUB CURVE EXAMPLE

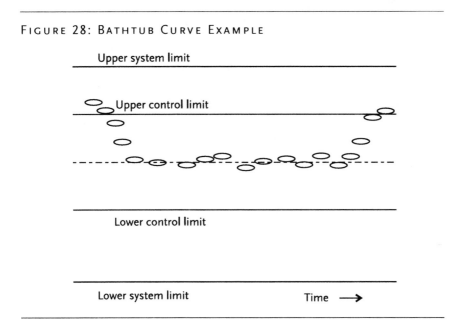

A mathematical distribution function actually exists that represents the bathtub curve; it is called the Weibull function, in honor of its inventor. Excel® even has it as a built-in function, WEIBULL(. . .).

The Null Hypothesis

Each trial will be designed to test whether the beneficial effect is gained. Because the old system had some variability and because the new system will have some variability, it is important that the trial be designed in such a way that the analyst can tell from the trial's data whether the effect is really there.

The designer of the trial poses a hypothesis. Suppose the analyst says, "The new average x-ray delivery time will be reduced by 20 minutes." This seems to be a sensible proposition, and gathering data about x-ray delivery times would likely provide a basis for evaluating the progress. There would be some variability, and that is to be expected.

To apply the tools of statistics to the evaluation of progress, it is necessary to cast the hypothesis in a form that statistics can address. This requires the application of a certain logic; this is done not because the logic is overwhelmingly attractive on its own merit but rather because it is the only logic that statisticians currently know how to analyze. Statistics is only about 100 years old, making it one of the youngest branches of mathematics; compare that with the geometry books that still do things the way Euclid did. Perhaps, in the next 100 years, a more appealing approach to the analysis of hypotheses will arise.

To apply the tools of statistics, the starting point is the *null hypothesis*. The null hypothesis states that there is no change. In our x-ray delivery case, the null hypothesis is that the average delivery time is not changed. The outcome of the trial will be one of two possibilities: the null hypothesis is supported or the null hypothesis is rejected.

However, allowance must be made for variability and uncertainty. Rather than a flat-out statement of support or rejection, the outcome will be stated with a certain degree of confidence, say 90 percent. The outcome will be stated, "With 90 percent confidence, the null hypothesis is supported (or rejected)."

Two special cases should be considered. Suppose that the data support the conclusion that the null hypothesis is to be rejected when in fact the underlying truth is that it should be supported. This is called a *false-negative* outcome. The opposite can also happen, and this is called a *false-positive* outcome. Both are of concern in the design and evaluation of any trial. It is not correct to jump to the conclusion that if the null hypothesis is not supported, the hypothesis must be accepted. There is a gray area where the data can support neither a positive nor a negative conclusion.

At the data analysis level, all trials boil down to being either a null-hypothesis test of the average value of a distribution or a null-hypothesis test of the standard deviation of a distribution, or perhaps both at the same time. Statistical analysis can only deal with these limited, numeric concepts. If statistical analysis is to be applied, the analyst must cast the trial into these limited terms.

Trial Duration

If the trial is to determine the reliability of a laboratory instrument having a mean-time-to-failure of five years, the trial is going to take a very long time. If the trial has to do with a medical event that is shown in historical records to happen once every month or so, the trial is going to take a number of months; if it is carried out for a shorter time than that, nobody is going to believe the result.

How much data will be enough? If the data are easy to get and are generated in huge quantities every day, the question is not very important. More data always support a clearer conclusion, so get more data if they are free. Unhappily, free and easily obtainable data are rarely found in the real world. Getting data takes time and effort, so knowing how much data will be required is a necessary part of the trial design process. Because time goes by while the data are being collected, having an idea of how many data samples are required bears directly on how long the trial will take.

The answer to the question, "How much data do we need?" depends on the confidence level required. If the confidence level is set at 75 percent, calculating a minimum data set size is possible. If the confidence level is set at 90 percent, more data will be needed, and if the confidence level is set at 95 percent, it will require even more data.

No absolute rule exists on what confidence level to set, but here are some general guidelines:

- Pick 75 percent if there is general enthusiasm for making the change anyway, the cost is not particularly great, and the downside risks are no greater than the risks associated with making no change.
- Pick 90 percent if general enthusiasm is mild, the cost is middling, and the downside risks are not negligible.
- Pick 95 percent if general enthusiasm is lacking, the cost of the change is high, or if particular downside risks are appreciable.

Trial Duration for Changes in the Average Value

The following procedure will produce the number of data points required to calculate the confidence interval about the average value, given a confidence level and a precision of result expressed in terms of the sample standard deviation.

Pick a confidence level, say 90 percent. Calculate the *significance level*, which is defined as one minus the confidence level; the significance level would be 10 percent, because the confidence level is 90 percent.

Make a rough guess of the number of data points, say 10. Then apply the Excel® function TINV(2 ∗ SIGNIFICANCE LEVEL, 10). (The built in function TINV(. . .) returns the two-tailed answer, whereas the one-tailed answer is sought. To force this to work, double the significance level. This probably sounds backward, but it is so.) For a significance level of 10 percent and a count estimate of 10, the function reads TINV(2 ∗ 10%, 10) and returns 1.37.

One more parameter needs to be specified by the analyst: the precision of the outcome desired by the analyst expressed as a fraction of the sample standard deviation. One-quarter of a standard deviation is a possibility, or one-half. Pick, say, one-quarter of a standard deviation. With that selection in hand, calculate the number of data points by dividing the TINV(. . .) result by the selected precision. In this case, that would be 1.37/0.25 = 5.49. Square this number; the square is an estimate of the number of data points required, in this case 30.13. Round that off to 30.

To confirm that the TINV(. . .) function does not depend very much on the number of samples supplied as an argument, the TINV(. . .) calculation can be repeated using 30 as the number of samples. Repeating the steps gives a TINV value of 1.31 and a calculated number of data points equal to 27.48, so the number of data samples hardly changes. This is only a planning estimate, and an estimate of 27 is hardly different from an estimate of 30.

Here is that same example worked step by step:

Estimating Average Value Trial Length

Confidence level	90%
Significance level	10%
Rough guess at data samples required	10
t-inverse value TINV(2 ∗ significance, rough guess)	1.37
Desired precision, fraction of sample standard deviation	0.25
That desired precision divided by the t-inverse value, in this case 0.25/1.37.	5.49
That value squared	30.13

(continued on following page)

New sample count estimate, which is the previous value rounded off	30
Optional second iteration, replacing the rough guess with this new estimate	—
t-inverse value TINV(2 ∗ significance, new estimate)	1.31
Precision divided by this t-inverse value, squared	27.48
Improved estimate of sample size (the above), rounded	27

This is a good enough estimate for trial planning purposes.

Note that a fairly modest number of data samples is required to support a high-confidence outcome; this is because average values are very well behaved. The table below covers a reasonable range of confidence levels and precision. Recall that precision is defined in standard deviation units, so a precision of 0.50 means that the sample average is within half a standard deviation of the true average.

Sample Size Required in Relation to Average Value

Confidence level	75%	90%	95%
Significance level	25%	10%	5%
Precision in standard deviation units			
1.00		3	4
0.50	3	8	13
0.25	8	27	45
0.10	46	166	272

Using this table and taking the same parameters as were used just above, in which the confidence level is 90 percent and the precision is 0.25 standard deviations, the table says the required sample size is 27, which agrees with the analysis above.

Sample Size for the Standard Deviation

If the purpose of the trial is to reduce the variability of a process, the trial needs to be run long enough to get a reasonable estimate of the new standard deviation. The development of a suitable sample size to estimate the distribution's standard deviation parallels the process used above to estimate the trial size when the average value is the primary interest, except that the chi-square distribution is used. The arithmetic is tedious, so it has been relegated to the web site that accompanies this book, www.ache.org/pubs/barry/start.cfm, and the resulting table of multipliers is given here in tabular form and covers the likely range of interest.

Sample Size Required in Relation to Standard Deviation

Confidence level	75%	90%	95%
Significance level	25%	10%	5%

Precision in standard deviation units			
1.00	6	9	12
0.50	13	27	37
0.25	45	90	125
0.10	275	500	750

To apply this principle, select a confidence level and a precision and then read the number of samples required. For example, if a confidence level of 90 percent and a precision of 25 percent of the sample standard deviation are selected, read 90 as the number of samples required.

It will be observed that, for the same confidence level and the same precision, more samples are required to determine the standard deviation than to determine the average value. Furthermore, to achieve a higher precision in the standard deviation requires many, many more samples.

The analyst is required to select a precision before looking up the sample count in the table. The precision is a multiplier on the standard deviation of the sample. However, at this point, the standard deviation of the future sample is not known. Even so, the precision method is reasonable. When the trials are run and the samples are collected, some uncertainty will remain in the answers, and that uncertainty will be related to the standard deviation of the sample.

Testing with Very Low Error Rates

Suppose we are tracking discrete events, some of which are errors. Let us further suppose that the error rate is very low. In testing processes with very low error rates, the trial may run for quite a long time with no errors found. If the old process had a low error rate, too, figuring out whether the new system is any better than the old one might be difficult. Suppose the error rate in the old process is one per 1,000 events. If the process handles 2,000 events per month, gathering a sample set that includes several errors will take a long time. If the new process being put through the trial is expected to have one error in a million events, the time spent completing the trial gets out of hand.

In the short run (during the trial), the question is whether the new system is in fact better than the old one. To answer this, a different distribution function will be brought to bear. An event that can have only one of two outcomes is called a *binomial* event. A binomial event has a probability of success and a probability of failure, and the sum of the two probabilities is unity.

Flip a coin. The probability of success in flipping heads is 50 percent, and the probability of *failing* to flip heads is 100 percent minus 50 percent, which equals 50 percent. Flip two coins at one time. The probability of success in flipping two heads is 25 percent, the probability of failing to flip two heads is 75 percent, and so on. Given a hat holding one red marble and two blue marbles, the probability of success in picking the red marble is 33.3 percent, and the probability of failure is 66.7 percent. What is the probability of flipping heads at least twice before flipping tails twice? Or of choosing the red marble twice before choosing one of the blue marbles?

Suppose the old system has a probability of success of 99.9 percent, which means that, on average, one error appears once in 1,000 cases. What is the likelihood of having 1,000 successes, 2,000 successes, or 3,000 successes before having *any* error?

Happily, built-in spreadsheet function is available that does this calculation; it is called the *negative binomial distribution*. In Excel®, the function is negbinomdist(number of preceding failures, number of successes, probability of success). The function returns the probability that exactly that number of failures will transpire before exactly that number of success given the probability of success.

Applying this function and specifying no failures and 3,000 successes calls for the spreadsheet formula to be NEGBINOMDIST(0, 3000, 99.9%), which returns 4.97 percent; we will call it 5 percent. If 5 percent is the probability of having *no* errors in the first 3,000 tries, the probability of having *at least one error* must be 95 percent. To fill out the picture, here are a few more points.

Tries before Any Failure	
Success Rate 99.9%	
Tries	Probability
1,000	36.8%
2,000	13.5%
3,000	5.0%
4,000	1.8%
5,000	0.7%
10,000	<0.1%

To summarize the table, the old system could be expected to have zero-error runs of 1,000 tries 37 percent of the time, zero-error runs of 3,000 tries only 5 percent of the time, and zero-error runs of 5,000 tries less than one percent of the time.

So, if the goal is to run the trial long enough to be 95 percent confident that the new system is better than the old one, the trial must be run long enough that the old system would be 95 percent likely to produce an error, which is about 3,000 tries. If the confidence level requirement is raised to 99 percent, the trial needs to run at about 5,000 tries. By that time, the old system would have, with 99 percent confidence, produced at least one error. If the new system produces none in that time, the new system is, with 99 percent confidence, better than the old one. How much better? The same NEGBINOMDIST(. . .) function can be applied on a trial-and-error basis to find out what the new process' error rate can be if the trial produces zero errors in the first run of 2,000 samples. Doing so gives the result that, with 75 percent confidence, the new process' error rate is not higher than 144 per million events. If the first 5,000 samples include no errors, the new process' error rate, with 75 percent confidence, is not higher than 60 per million events.

Testing the Hypothesis

Test the hypothesis by running the trial long enough to generate a sufficient number of samples, and analyze the results. The standard statistical tests that are available are the t-test for the average value and the F-test for the standard deviation. These answer the questions, "Is the average still the same after the process change, and with what confidence?" and "Is the standard deviation still the same after the process change, and with what confidence?" With a spreadsheet such as Excel®, these tests are easy to apply. However, both are rather conservative tests and may be frustrating in real applications.

What is more rewarding is to track progress with control charts. Although the eye may be fooled by distributions that are nearly the same, the eye is not likely to be fooled if a significant change is seen between the old process and the new one. If the improvement is so small that the eye is fooled, there is no point in studying this candidate change any further; it is not worth the bother.

FIGURE 29: TRACKING CHART—THE TRIAL BEGINS

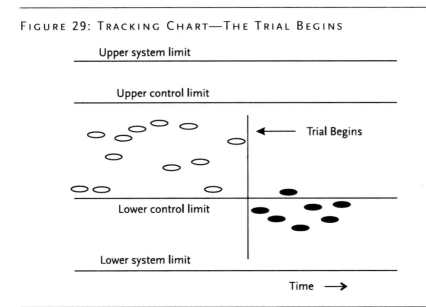

In this control chart, some of the data from the old system data are included for reference, and the old process control limits and system limits are shown. The start of the trial is marked, and the new data are plotted on the same chart, using a color highlight. In this case, the data are clearly clustering at a lower point on the page and, so far, seem to be more closely bunched.

When 20 or so new data points are available, new control charts can be generated with new control limits and new system limits. The spreadsheet functions TTEST(. . .) and FTEST(. . .) can be applied to complement the visual inspection of progress.

Factorial Experiments

A factorial experimental series is one in which two or more changes are considered in various combinations. In a factory, various machine setting combinations can be tried and the best ones selected for production.

In a healthcare organization, setting up combinatorial testing is practically impossible; it is too complicated, and it takes too long. Other outside influences are likely to fog the data. In actuality, the issue is rather the reverse. In healthcare, variable factors are involved that cannot be eliminated. If the health service runs 24 hours a day, the effect of which shift is being studied might be important to the outcome of the trial; so might weekend versus weekday; so might patient care unit variation. Just listing these built-in combinations gives us something approaching a factorial experiment.

There is a simple way to organize these combinations and to extract some information from them, particularly identifying those variables that seem to have a large influence on the results. This information may make it possible to isolate the key variables for further study.

Here is an example. A hospital wants to know if adding more paraprofessional staff to the patient care units will decrease the time it takes to deliver the mid-shift medication to each patient. One would hope so, but a Scottish dictum tells us, "One boy is a boy, two boys are less than a boy, and three boys are no boy at all." The three patient care units and four shifts during the week provide a lot of variables to ponder. Also, the hospital wonders if striking a gong at the mid-shift hour would get the medication round started on time and, perhaps, ended on time. Data are gathered, with the following outcomes:

Gong	Paras	Shift 1	Shift 2	Shift 3	Time
−1	1	1	−1	−1	34.0
−1	2	1	−1	−1	27.0
−1	3	1	−1	−1	23.0
−1	1	−1	1	−1	27.0
−1	2	−1	1	−1	25.0
−1	3	−1	1	−1	23.0

(continued on following page)

Gong	Paras	Shift 1	Shift 2	Shift 3	Time
−1	1	−1	−1	1	21.0
−1	2	−1	−1	1	20.0
−1	3	−1	−1	1	19.0
−1	1	−1	−1	−1	41.0
−1	2	−1	−1	−1	38.0
−1	3	−1	−1	−1	33.0
1	1	1	−1	−1	17.0
1	2	1	−1	−1	13.5
1	3	1	−1	−1	11.5
1	1	−1	1	−1	13.5
1	2	−1	1	−1	12.5
1	3	−1	1	−1	11.5
1	1	−1	−1	1	10.5
1	2	−1	−1	1	10.0
1	3	−1	−1	1	9.5
1	1	−1	−1	−1	20.5
1	2	−1	−1	−1	19.0
1	3	−1	−1	−1	16.5

The heading "Paras" is the number of paraprofessionals on the patient care unit. The entries under "Gong" and the different shifts are numeric values implying "no" and "yes"; any numeric values would do. For the shifts, if Shift 1 is true, then Shifts 2 and 3 are false, and so on.

With numeric values in every square, regression analysis takes over. Using spreadsheet regression and identifying time as the y-value and the five other columns as x-values, the regression tool creates the relationship between variables and outcomes. The fitted equation has a coefficient for each of the variables, and every coefficient is accompanied by a confidence interval.

As has now been shown many times in this book, if only a few sample data points are available, the confidence intervals are so wide as to be useless. Take that as a true message: there is a great uncertainty in the fitted values. Let us put the fitted coefficients aside and look at another output from the analysis.

In Excel®, if the box LINE-FIT CHARTS is checked on the REGRESSION panel, the program will produce several simple charts, each of which show the given data points and the fitted points. Here's the chart for the gong variable. Dependence on the gong variable is shown by the data points on the left (no gong) being substantially higher on the page than the points on the right (yes gong). Looking at the other plots, which can be found on the web site that accompanies this book, www.ache.org/pubs/barry/start.cfm, one sees much less dependence on those other variables.

FIGURE 30: GONG LINE-FIT PLOT

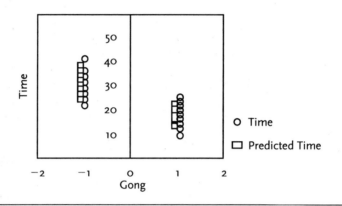

Thus the regression analysis provides the service of organizing these simple data charts, which facilitate screening the important variables away from the less important variables. A statistician may be able to glean the same information from the many statistical characteristics provided by the analysis, but there is nothing in those numbers that is not obvious to the eye in these charts.

Note that there is no requirement that every combination be covered in the table; what is required is that a numeric value be given in each case to represent true or false, as was done with the gong variable above. If some squares are blank, leave out those rows. It is left to the reader to decide whether the idea that a gong gets everybody moving constitutes useful management guidance.

An Integrated Example

This example is not taken from any real experience nor does it imply in any way that such things could happen in any healthcare organization. This example is offered because it shows the Six Sigma approach to analyzing important situations and can be understood by the lay reader.

The Event

A staff nurse prepares to inject a patient with a prescribed drug. At the last moment, the nurse pauses to consider whether the dosage seems to be reasonable. Upon reflection, the nurse decides that the dosage is much too great, stops the injection, and notifies management and the attending physician through established channels.

The Standing Procedure

Although many medications come in "adult" and "child" sizes, others are prescribed in proportion to the patient's body weight, typically in milligrams per kilogram of body weight. Digoxin and some other drugs are prescribed in milligrams for adults and micrograms per kilogram of body weight for infants.

A physician prescribes the medication. If the medication is prescribed according to body weight, the physician uses the body weight from the patient's record, does the arithmetic, and decides on the quantity of medicine for the patient. If the physician prescribes this particular medicine frequently, the unit quantities are immediately available to him by rote; if this physician prescribes this particular medicine infrequently, a reference book is consulted for the quantities. A charge nurse notes the prescribed dose and duplicates the calculations. If there is agreement between the physician's and nurse's calculations, the order is sent to the pharmacy.

The pharmacist receives the pharmacy order, checks the prescribed medicine against the patient's known allergies and against other medication this patient is known to be taking, and checks the dosage against the patient's body weight. The patient information is taken from the patient's record. If no conflict is found, the pharmacist fills the order and sends it to the patient care unit.

A staff nurse in the patient care unit checks the delivery from the pharmacy against the original physician's prescription and delivers the medicine to the patient. The staff nurse also considers whether the dose seems to be consistent with the patient's body weight.

Action

Hospital management assigns a project sponsor from the senior management ranks. The sponsoring senior manager selects a Six Sigma black belt to lead the project. The project leader meets with the line managers from the concerned departments and conveys management's directive that the issue be resolved and management's request that all parties provide full cooperation and support. The sponsoring senior manager confirms that this is management's position, giving each person present a firm look in the eye.

The project leader asks if anyone remembers other similar cases in the past year or so. Two or three people mention cases that, although they were not exactly the same, they remember being in the same ballpark. The group concludes that this case cannot be declared unique. The group also agrees that the same might recur at any time and, because of this, that some stop-gap mechanism should be applied immediately. The group performs a fishbone analysis to identify likely causes and to make sure the entire group has a common understanding of the issues.

The group agrees that the hospital records should be examined for comparable events. The patient care staff should be encouraged to recollect comparable events. Procedures from comparable hospitals should be examined to provide a benchmark against which the present process as well as any candidate future process can be tested.

Stop-Gap Measures

Given the serious nature of the issue, the group considers that some stop-gap measures need to be put in place and applied until a full analysis can be completed. The stop-gap measures will break the chain of events. The group recognizes that any stop-gap measure will add to operating expense and may well slow down the nominal processing times. Given the gravity of the issue, the group considers that management will support the stop-gap measures.

The group considers what measures to apply. After some discussion, the group settles on inserting one additional check of the medication order at the patient care unit, after the pharmacy order is delivered to the patient care unit and before the medicine delivery round is started. This check will be done by a registered nurse, and the check will be included in the patient's record as well as in a project log.

The group considers the potential problems with this measure, which are captured in the management-level chart shown here.

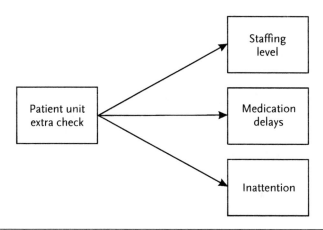

The recognized potential problems are these:

1. The extra workload on the staff nurses needs to be considered, and it may be necessary to add a nurse per patient care unit during this stop-gap period.
2. The time taken to do the extra checking after the pharmacy order is delivered means that there will be some additional delay before the round can begin. Because it may take half an hour to do the checking, the delay can bunch work up and interfere with other duties.
3. The routine nature of this overchecking may become so mechanical that the person doing the overchecking does not give full attention to the task, thereby following the bathtub failure model.

After some discussion, the group revises the plan to take care of these potential problems:

1. The overcheck will not be done after the pharmacy order is delivered; rather, the overcheck will be done between the time the physician gives the order and the time the pharmacy delivers the order, working from the pharmacy order and the patient's record. This will not catch errors made in the pharmacy, but the group considers these the least likely. The group judges that one or two nurses

per shift can do the overchecking for all patient care units, moving from unit to unit. The patient care unit head nurse will do the overchecking for those exceptional cases where time so requires.

2. A senior nursing supervisor will spot-check the overchecks on a sample basis to keep the attention level high.
3. The staff nurse, before delivering the medication, will check both the original physician's order and the overcheck entry in the patient's record.
4. All errors of every kind will be reported to the project office so that a data record can be accumulated.
5. The overcheck nurses will report on their experience to the project office and provide timely reports to line management.
6. The project leader will walk the floors from time to time to gather anecdotal input from patient care unit personnel, pharmacy personnel, physicians, and others—indeed, information will be collected from anyone who has anything to say.

Gathering the Data

Patient records are studied for the prior 20 months, which is the longest period of time for which the records are reasonably available. This study shows that the error rate is about one per 1,000 when all manner of similar errors are considered. Few if any of these errors were actually life-threatening, but the point of the study is to gather information about how the system works.

The data are these:

Month	Error Rate per 1,000	Month	Error Rate per 1,000
June	2.1	May	1.1
July	0.4	June	0.3
August	0.6	July	1.3
September	1.7	August	1.5
October	0.4	September	1.3
November	0.5	October	1.2
December	0	November	0.5
January	1.0	December	1.2
February	0.2	January	0.7
March	1.4	**Average**	**1.0**
April	2.1	**Standard deviation**	**0.8**

From these data, the analyst calculates Six Sigma system limits at zero on the lower side and average-plus-six-times-the-standard-deviation on the upper side, which is to say 5.8 errors per 1,000. The process control limits, which are three standard deviations away from the average value, are at zero and 3.4 errors per 1,000.

The analyst considers subgroups of the data and finds no appreciable dependence on shift, patient care unit, patient age category, common drug versus uncommon drug, or any other parameter anyone in the group could imagine. The error rate is low in all cases, so the sample size in the subgroups is too low to provide much guidance.

Assessing the Stop-Gap Measures

The project leader calls a meeting of the group. The analyst presents the information and the system limits. Upon discussion, the group decides that the previously prescribed stop-gap measures will cover the range from zero to six errors per 1,000. The group and the leader recommend the following to management:

1. that the stop-gap measures be continued until further notice
2. that any concomitant changes in staffing, work scheduling, or standard costs be made permanent
3. that data gathering continue
4. that the opinion of the group is that the hospital has a system weakness, as the problem cannot be localized
5. that consideration be given to changes in the system that would provide a substantial reduction in the error rate

Implications of the Six Sigma System Limits

With the stop-gap measures in place, the group believes that the error rate will be much lower than the previous one per 1,000, although not yet enough data are in hand to say that the error rate will be as low as 3.4 per million. Performance will be tracked and, as data are accumulated, the error rate will be quantified.

The stop-gap efforts add extra nursing effort and therefore add to operating cost. The stop-gap efforts, by allowing time for a replacement pharmacy order if necessary, dilate the time required to complete the pharmacy order process. Both of these are negatives.

This issue can be considered in two parts. The added nursing effort is internal to the process; it now costs more to do this process. The time dilation is external to the process and affects the overall system. Other parties need to adjust their schedules to accommodate the time dilation. A change in system limits always affects other parties.

The group believes that the added cost and the changed system limits, even with their effects on other parties, are the correct management action to take in the short run because the pharmacy order error rate will be brought down substantially. The group asks management to accept the cost and the other parties to accept the changed system limits.

The group now pursues improvement of the cost and the system limits by seeking other sufficient solutions. This means that the group will only consider changes to the process that will have error rates on the order of 3.4 per million and that it will not consider changes that save money and time but that do not reduce the error rate to approximately 3.4 per million.

Failure Modes and Effects Analysis

The pre-existing system had four checks in series: the physician checked his or her own work, the attending nurse calculated the dosage independently, the pharmacist calculated the dosage independently, and the patient care unit nurse checked the delivered medication against the original order and against common practice. For the wrong dosage to reach the patient, four independent failures had to happen.

To visualize the process, look for common sources of error, and identify weak spots in the process, failure mode and effects charts are prepared by the analyst working with nurses, pharmacists, and physicians from the project group.

FIGURE 32: DOSAGE FAILURE MODE ANALYSIS

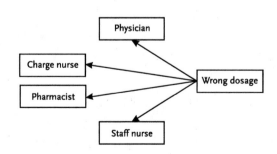

For each of the actors, an additional failure mode and effects chart was produced by the same group. The charts for the charge nurse and the pharmacist look the same, so just one will be included here.

FIGURE 33: FAILURE MODE CHART FOR THE PHYSICIAN

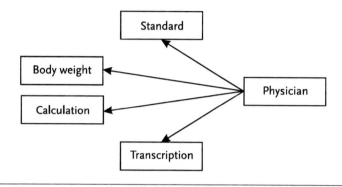

FIGURE 34: FAILURE MODE CHART FOR THE CHARGE NURSE

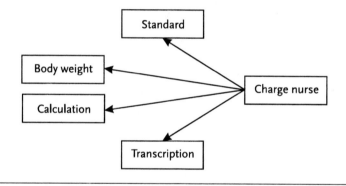

The chart for the patient care unit staff nurse is a little different.

FIGURE 35: FAILURE MODE CHART FOR THE STAFF NURSE

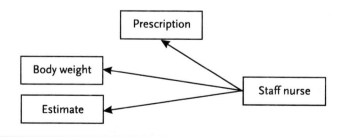

The four charts clearly indicate that there is one candidate for common-mode error: the body weight.

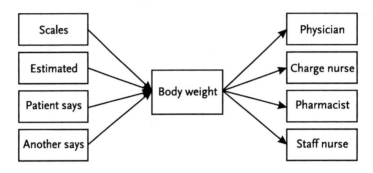

Further investigation reveals that the hospital routinely weighs infants and small children, and there is no reason to believe that the scales are unreliable. Ambulatory adults are weighed, but non-ambulatory patients may or may not be weighed. If the adult patient is not weighed, the staff either make an estimate based on experience or ask the patient or an accompanying family member for estimated weight. The group believes that the estimates are probably within 20 percent, that the patient is probably accurate within 20 percent, and that the weight guessed by an accompanying family member is very imprecise.

The data show that in at least one case of interest, the patient was a small child who had been weighed at the hospital on standard scales. So, although this is a weak spot in the system, it cannot be the only one.

No other common sources of error connect to all four actors, but there is one that connects the physician and the attending nurse: the calculation and transcription act. Although the charge nurse is trained to provide an independent calculation and transcription, anecdotal information tells the group that the nurses are subject to distraction and they are more likely to believe the doctor's calculations than their own. In other words, the independent check is not completely independent.

The pharmacist is completely independent in that he or she does separate calculations away from the bedside. Indeed, some of the included cases in the database are errors caught by the pharmacist. The patient care unit staff nurse does not do a calculation but relies only on experience and training to recognize unusual cases. The staff nurse does check the pharmacy order against the pharmacy delivery.

Three-Plane Modeling

The group elected to consider the three-plane portrayal of the situation to see if any conditions or constraints need further attention. The main elements, in the group's opinion, are shown in the following table:

Three-Plane Model of the Pharmacy Order Issue

Mechanisms	Conditions	Constraints
Physician prescribes medicine	Patient's weight often estimated, not measured	Manual bedside system; pharmacist has computer cross-check facility
Charge nurse confirms	Charge nurses tend to discount their own calculations and accept the physician's	Policy is to weigh patients, but there is no way to do so for bedfast patients and some emergency patients
Pharmacist checks	Pharmacist works from patient's record	Manual order-writing system; manual bedside cross-checking system
Staff nurse considers	Physician may make decimal error or call up wrong dose from memory	System is an open loop, with no feedback to the physician or charge nurse before drug is given to patient
	Staff nurse will catch gross errors on familiar drugs but probably not those on less-familiar drugs	No peer review of physician's prescription

The group finds the three-plane portrayal interesting because the constraints plane identifies those matters that management will wish to address in the longer term. Management cannot do much about the conditions, but it can change the constraints. The group takes note that the constraints plane has one new matter: peer review (or rather the lack of peer review) of the physician's prescription. The group decides, after discussing the matter, that this is too far afield, because the charge to the group is to deal with errors downstream of the diagnosis. This may be a suitable topic for later, separate consideration or for research into computer-supported bedside diagnosis methods or other future technology.

Group's Conclusions

The group draws the following conclusions:

1. The hospital should weigh all patients who receive weight-dependent medication.
2. The hospital should provide independent bedside calculation and transcription of pharmacy orders.
3. Emphasis should be given to adding technology to address the conditions rather than to adding manual checking or other manual steps.

The group recommends that practices of comparable hospitals be reviewed, vendors be contacted, and suitable trials of candidate changes be undertaken. It also recommends continuing the data gathering and the stop-gap measures until further notice.

Management Action

Hospital management issues an order that all patients be weighed as part of the admitting process. For those patients who must be medicated before it is possible to weigh them, the hospital orders that caution be used in prescribing weight-dependent medication and that the patient be weighed at the first opportunity, with confirmation of any intervening medication dosage.

Hospital management authorizes the project leader to undertake trials to find better systems for precluding bedside calculation and transcription errors.

Trial of a Handheld Device

From various vendor offerings, the project leader, in consultation with the group, selects a handheld computer device with a small screen and wand. The handheld computer contains data on 400 medications including standard dosage, adult dosage, infant dosage, weight-dependent dosage, and the like. The device does not have a printer, but it retains all information, which can be transferred to a personal computer at the patient care unit station at the end of the round. The device's wand is a barcode reader that picks up the patient's barcode from his or her record. The wand also acts as a stylus so that the user can interact with the handheld device to select a medication, enter a body weight, and so on.

A question then arises: Should both the physician and the charge nurse have one of these devices, or should just the physician or just the nurse have one? After consulting with physicians and nurses, the project leader decides that, for the first trial, the charge nurse would be issued the handheld device rather than the physician. The physician would continue to make calculations in the traditional way.

Two patient care units are selected for the trial. A total of ten handheld devices are acquired. The vendor provides additional on-site support during the trial in hopes of winning an eventual order for more substantial quantities.

Trial Duration

The current error rate is one per 1,000 pharmacy orders. The hospital has 200 acute care beds plus an outpatient service, so the number of pharmacy orders is about 2,000 per month.

The analyst believes that there is general support for a change in the direction of a handheld device because the hospital is evaluating electronic records and other data-automation concepts and the staff are generally interested in computer devices. The handheld devices are not burdensomely expensive. Therefore, the analyst believes that the trial should be designed to a confidence level of 75 percent.

The trial should endure until the new average value is determined to a precision of about half a standard deviation. The table provided in an earlier chapter of this book leads the analyst to conclude that about 3,000 samples of pharmacy orders will be required. At the current rate of 2,000 pharmacy orders per month, it would take about six weeks to get 3,000 samples if the whole hospital were involved in the trial. Upon inspection, it is decided that the two patient care units being tested generate about one-third of the total pharmacy orders, so to get a total of

3,000 pharmacy orders from these two patient care units will take about ten weeks.

The old system had some months with no errors. Because this is true, there is a reasonable likelihood that the two patient care units, using the old system, would have periods of ten weeks with no errors at all. Therefore, running with no errors for two or three months may or may not provide sufficient evidence that the new system is actually better than the old system; some analysis is required. Applying the negative binomial distribution to determine the likelihood that 3,000 successful outcomes will happen before the first error gives the likelihood of about 5 percent. So, under the old system, any 3,000 successive pharmacy orders will have at least one error, with a likelihood of 95 percent; the analyst can be 95 percent confident that, if no errors are found in the first 3,000 pharmacy orders during the trial, the new system is an improvement over the old system. This result is better than the 75 percent confidence level requirement set by the analyst, so it is accepted.

Thus, the trial evaluation method will be as follows:

1. Run the trial until the trial patient care units have issued 3,000 pharmacy orders, which will be about ten weeks.
2. Expect no errors during that time.
3. If even one error occurs during the trial, the new system cannot be shown to be better than the old system.

Trial Execution

Nurses were selected from among a group of volunteers, and general cooperation by the physicians was granted. The nurses were trained on the new device.

The nurses did a potential problem analysis, which involved considering the following: any ripple effects of carrying one more device on the rounds; the responsibility for transferring the patient data from the handheld device to the patient care unit computer at the end of the rounds; the responsibility to print out the patient data sheet and include it in the patient's record; and the question of whether the nurse's signature should be affixed to the printed form or if the nurse's name entered into the handheld device would be sufficient. Questions of battery replacement and what to do if the device gets lost or damaged were aired.

The hospital's information technology department assigned one person to be the go-to person for any problems with the handheld device. The vendor's on-site representative pledged to be available immediately, or at least promptly, in response to a page.

A pretrial period of three days was declared, during which the nurses would use the handheld device just to get the hang of it, with no entries going into patient records. This was intended to address the likely "infant mortality" errors as people got used to the new devices.

The trial ran for ten weeks. No errors were observed. Nurses found that the handheld devices could be carried in a pocket without much bother. The data transfer at the end of the round was taken over by the patient care unit clerk. Nurses adopted the habit of checking the patient's record on the next round to be sure that the calculation record was there. Physicians got in the habit of checking the handheld device for dose standards for drugs not commonly used, just to verify their recollection of the standards.

Nurses found that they sometimes made an error in putting the body weight into the handheld device, most commonly a decimal error, but since this calculation was completely independent of the physician's calculation, the discrepancy was immediately noted in every such event and corrected on the spot. This was not counted as an error because it did not increase the risk to the patient. Two handheld devices were lost or damaged during the trial. These were replaced from the inventory of spares.

In walking the floors to talk to the people involved, the Six Sigma project leader received 27 suggestions for other features the handheld device might have to make it more useful to the users. These were logged for future evaluation.

Long-Term Tracking

Tracking of the pharmacy order error rate continues over the long term to make sure that the process does not degrade over time. A periodic report is created that flows to the affected parties and to management.

Cost-Benefit Analysis

The cost-benefit analysis compares two sufficient solutions: the stopgap solution and the new-technology solution. The lease cost for the handheld devices is found to be less than five dollars per day per patient care unit. The stop-gap cost of extra nursing effort is found to be fifty dollars per day per patient care unit. On the basis of cost alone, the new-technology solution is preferred.

The time dilation, which is represented by the system limits that go with the stop-gap measures, is not easily expressed in dollar terms. Therefore, the comparison between the stop-gap and the new-technology solutions has to be expressed in nonmonetary terms. The new-technology solution allows the system limits to be revised to reflect the removal of the time dilation, which is favorable. Therefore, the cost analysis and the system limits improvements both favor the new-technology solution.

There would be no point in attempting to apply a cost-benefit analysis to a change from the old process to any new process because the old process (without the stop-gap measures) was unacceptable, no matter how favorable its costs. Cost-benefit analysis is appropriate only when comparing sufficient solutions.

Conclusion of the Event

At the end of the trial period, the project leader met with the group once again. Upon discussion of the information received, the group recommended the following:

1. that the handheld device trial be considered a success and that it be extended to the balance of the hospital in an orderly progression, with due consideration for special circumstances such as the emergency room service
2. that the data logging be continued and periodic reports be issued to management and to interested parties
3. that the patient care unit level overchecking be discontinued as the handheld device use extends to the whole of the hospital and that the nurses doing the overchecking work be reassigned
4. that the several suggestions for added functionality be circulated for consideration by interested parties with no commitment at this stage
5. that, although the body-weight estimation issue seems to have caused no errors during the trial period, further consideration be given to finding ways to weigh bedfast or otherwise hard-to-weigh

adult and adolescent patients and that the responsibility for this be assigned to an appropriate senior staff member for resolution

6. that the project report be filed and the project case be closed
7. that the senior management express its thanks to the many people who participated in making the trial a success

SIX SIGMA: CONCLUSION

Performance of the System Is What Counts

To get the system to work well, it is necessary to get the employees to work well and to get management to manage well. Employees work well when the tasks they do are designed under the poka-yoke guidelines and the work flows in a sensible way. Management manages well when facts are organized and information is quantified, when problems get solved, when new problems are detected before they are serious, and when change is managed. Both management and employees respond to worthy goals.

Six Sigma, by setting the worthy goal of 3.4 errors per million opportunities, applying poka-yoke guidelines to the design of work tasks, providing systematic problem-solving and problem-detecting methods, and providing a systematic, quantitative method for managing change, is a worthwhile management method with useful applicability to health-care.

PART II

Cases

These cases are provided for those readers who wish to apply the lessons of the book. In particular, readers following a Six Sigma training program with a Six Sigma trainer to achieve green belt or black belt certification will find the cases organized to help them achieve their goals.

The cases introduce additional material to extend mastery beyond what has been provided in the text of the book.

A few extra cases appear at the end that are mental exercises for those who wish to delve deeper into workflow analysis. Although the primary case studies all deal directly with healthcare situations, these workflow cases deal with the management issues of running an amusement park. The reader may find them interesting and amusing.

CASE INSTRUCTIONS

Each case addresses material that may arise in the practice of the Six Sigma method. Because Six Sigma projects are always of keen interest to management, the report for each case is to be organized as if it was to be presented to management. Because management personnel have notoriously short attention spans, each report is to be organized as a slide show in Microsoft PowerPoint® or an equivalent application. Each report will have the following:

- a cover slide stating the name and purpose of the project or case
- a bulleted slide stating the key points being addressed (a bulleted slide has short text statements listed, with a bullet, as shown here, to add drama)

- a few information slides, preferably graphics
- a bulleted slide stating conclusions
- a bulleted slide stating any management actions being recommended

There are sample slideshows for representative cases on the companion web site at www.ache.org/pubs/barry/start.cfm. The web site also includes PowerPoint® templates that may be used as a starting point for designing suitable presentations for these reports.

In your report, use the spellchecker, think about the style, and make it look good. Presentation is not everything, but respectful consideration of the audience is good manners. Senior management is used to seeing polished presentations and cannot help but judge accordingly.

Clip art can be added to some slides to lighten the tone, but this should be done judiciously. Clip art slides will get more attention than text slides, which can be good if the clip art reinforces the message. Alternatively, clip art will distract the audience and obliterate the message you are trying to deliver if it is not precisely on point.

The Green Belt Series of Cases

Six Sigma green belt certification asserts that the certified green belt holder is competent to carry out Six Sigma projects. The first ten cases apply Six Sigma principles. The trainer for a green belt class may wish to assign these first ten cases. The trainer may also assign a special project to each student, or, for variety, he or she may substitute other cases that cover the same material.

Many of these cases include data sets. The data sets are provided in Excel® format on the companion web site, www.ache.org/pubs/barry/start.cfm, to save the student from tedious keying.

The Black Belt Series of Cases

Six Sigma black belt certification asserts that the certified black belt holder is competent to design Six Sigma projects and to supervise their execution. The trainer for a black belt class may wish to assign the green belt series and, in addition, cases 11 through 20. The trainer will also assign a special project to each student that will include the design and execution of a trial. For variety, the trainer may substitute other cases that cover the same material.

Excel® Use

These cases require a spreadsheet computer application such as Microsoft Excel®. Those who do not have prior experience using a spreadsheet would benefit from doing a tutorial series before starting these cases. Tutorials are commonly provided with the application and may be found by selecting the help menu and searching for "tutorial." If no tutorial is readily at hand, please look into the "ice-breaker" Excel® file on the companion web site, www.ache.org/pubs/barry/start.cfm. The ice-breaker exercises cover all of the fundamental spreadsheet operations that are required to do the cases. As with most computer applications, asking questions of a more experienced user is productive; although the operations are simple enough once they are known, they are baffling to the first-time user.

The Companion Web Site

The companion web site, www.ache.org/pubs/barry/start.cfm, includes the following:

1. an Excel® template containing all of the case input data for each case
2. an Excel® file providing additional details on the examples used in the text and in the appendix
3. PowerPoint® presentation templates
4. two completed case reports for general guidance
5. an ice-breaker spreadsheet

The Excel® files are in "template" format. The user can load these files, make entries, and save the resulting file as an Excel® spreadsheet model. The template file remains pristine and can be used again *de novo*. A trainer may wish to make various modifications and additions to these templates and save the result as a new template file, using the "save as . . ." feature.

Slide Showmanship

Those proficient in the creation and delivery of slide show presentations may choose to skip this section. Others may find benefit in spending a few minutes here.

Style

The specific directions here are for Microsoft PowerPoint®; the directions for other applications will be slightly different but largely similar to these.

Select a template for the PowerPoint® presentation; two are offered for your consideration on the companion web site, www.ache.org/pubs/barry/start.cfm. The quickest way to get started is to navigate to the template using Windows Explorer® and then to double-click on the template file name. PowerPoint® templates have a ".ppt" file tag. Alternatively, launch PowerPoint®, choose TEMPLATE from the first panel presented to you, and then choose either the tab GENERAL or the tab PRESENTATION DE-SIGNS. Select a template you like. Many organizations have their own standard template. If you have a free choice, pick a simple style with a lot of contrast between text and background so that the presentation will be easy to read in a standard conference room.

Select menu VIEW, then MASTER, and then SLIDE MASTER. Set up the footers for all slides by selecting menu VIEW, then HEADERS & FOOTERS. Enter the project name in the footer text box. Enter the presentation date in the date box, and uncheck the automatic date changer. Check DON'T SHOW ON THE TITLE SLIDE. Close by selecting APPLY TO ALL SLIDES. Edit the slide master by adding the organization's logo or other such touches.

Double-check the look of the title slide; that is the one that everybody will surely see. Select menu VIEW, then MASTER, and then TITLE MASTER. If any graphics do not show up here, add them again. Make any other changes considered necessary on the title slide. Save and close this slide.

Now you are ready to deal with the meat of the presentation. Select VIEW, then select SLIDE. The title slide will appear. Enter the name of the project as the title, and enter the team members' names as the subtitle. Save the slide.

Select menu INSERT, and then select NEW SLIDE. Select a bulleted slide. Use the bulleted list to state the purpose of the project in a very few lines. Save this slide.

Select menu INSERT, then NEW SLIDE. Select a chart slide. Enter a title. Copy and paste a chart from the spreadsheet or the graphics application. To paste, the general rule is to use PASTE SPECIAL, PICTURE. Save this new slide.

Select menu INSERT, and again select NEW SLIDE. Select a chart or bulleted format and make up as many additional slides as necessary to cover the material you need to cover. Save each slide.

End with a bulleted slide that gives recommendations to management. Tell management what you want them to do. They may decide to do something else, but you, as the best-informed person in the room, owe them your advice on the matter.

Select menu VIEW, and then select SLIDE SORTER. Look at the slides in sequence, and move them around as necessary to give the right flow to the presentation. Save any changes that you make.

Select menu VIEW, then SLIDE SHOW. Run through the whole presentation. Take notes, and then go back to the SLIDE SORTER and select slides that require editing. Run the slide show again. Save any changes that you make.

Use transition effects and progressive-build effects sparingly. Use the speaker's notes feature rather than writing notes on your shirt cuff. Keep the details in the speaker's notes, not on the slides. Get to the speaker's notes view by selecting menu VIEW and then selecting SPEAKER'S NOTES. . . .

The Presentation

The following rules for a successful presentation are tried and true:

1. Stand to the side of the screen, not next to the projector.
2. Use a stick pointer, and use it sparingly. Laser pointers have too much jitter and should be used only if the screen is so big that a stick pointer will not reach.
3. Plan for two minutes per slide, and make the slide count fit the time budget. Timeliness shows respect. Leave plenty of time for management to discuss things at the end of the presentation and for management to give instructions to the team.
4. Look your audience in the eye. If all eyes are not on the screen, go to the next slide.

5. Do not read the slide to the audience. Rather, give the audience a few seconds to read the slide, then point out and explain one main feature on the slide and move on. When you speak, turn to face the audience so that your voice will carry.

6. If you keep the slides moving, you will have the best chance of keeping questions on the point, and you may even get most of the questions at the end, when you can best answer them in context. However, if a question is asked, answer it briefly and move on.

7. Keep looking the audience in the eye. They are watching the screen, and you are watching them.

8. At the end, pause and invite response from the management present. Answer any questions briefly. Call on team members to answer specific questions when appropriate. Invite management to speak before time runs out. When instructions are given to you and to the team, write them down and repeat them back to make sure you understand them.

The audience for a Six Sigma project presentation will very likely include higher reaches of management than the presenter deals with on a daily basis. Senior management spends a lot of time thinking about succession planning and has but few opportunities to interact with those outside their immediate circle. Make the most of this opportunity. If the team has a clothing motif, such as a project jacket, dress the way the team dresses. Otherwise, dress the way management dresses.

CASE 1: DATA PORTRAYAL

Drill on Applying Six Sigma

Cases 1, 2, and 3 are a set. In these cases, the basic Six Sigma data portrayal and analysis are applied to the data sets provided. The standard spreadsheet tools are applied.

Topic: Tool Drill

These days, most personal computers have a sufficient set of tools to facilitate the data analysis and portrayal that are necessary parts of Six Sigma projects. This first case applies those tools to the set of data provided below. The data set is provided in computer form on the companion web site, www.ache.org/pubs/barry/start.cfm.

Those who have no prior experience with a spreadsheet computer application would do well to run through a tutorial. If no tutorial is readily available, the novice may wish to work through the ice-breaker Excel® sheet on the web site that accompanies this book, which walks through the fundamentals. Because this ice breaker is limited in scope, doing a complete tutorial at the first opportunity is a good idea.

A complete solution to this case is also provided on the web site.

Work

1. Calculate the average and the standard deviation for the data set using the built-in functions AVERAGE(. . .) and STDEV(. . .).
2. Calculate the process control limits, which are defined as three standard deviations above and below the average. Make two new columns on the spreadsheet and copy these limits into those columns so that one column is all upper process control limit and the other is all lower control limit. These will be used for plotting. These cells will have one column for the upper limit, the cells of which have the same value, and one column for the lower limit, the cells of which have the same value.
3. Calculate the system limits, which are at six standard deviations above and below the average. If the lower limit goes below zero, use zero as the lower limit. Make a column on the spreadsheet for the lower system limit and the upper system limit, as above. The upper limit cells will all have the same value. The lower limit cells will all have the same value.
4. Plot a scatter diagram, which is made up of points not connected by lines. Select all the data columns, including the counter column. Select menu INSERT, then CHART, then choose the SCATTER DIAGRAM option, and follow the rest of the instructions. Include the data, the process control limits, and the system limits, which will all show up as dots. Finish this chart.

   Using the completed chart, change the upper process control limit to a line. To do this, right-click on one of the upper process control limit points on the graph to get a pop-up menu. Select

FORMAT DATA SERIES. In the left panel entitled LINE, select AUTOMATIC. In the right panel entitled MARKER, select NONE. Close the menu. Repeat this process for the other limit lines.

5. Save the spreadsheet with a suitable name.

Create a histogram of the data. Select menu TOOLS, then DATA ANALYSIS, and then HISTOGRAM. If the TOOLS menu does not show DATA ANALYSIS on its list, it is necessary to activate DATA ANALYSIS before it can be used. This is easy to do. Start again; select TOOLS, then ADD-INS, and then ANALYSIS TOOLPAK. Close this menu. Select menu TOOLS again, and the DATA ANALYSIS option will appear at the bottom of the list.

The HISTOGRAM tool requires that the user identify the bins that the tool will drop the data into. Create a column of bins starting at zero and running to 3.0 in steps of 0.1. The first few entries will be 0, 0.1, 0.2, 0.3, and so on. Run the HISTOGRAM tool.

Caution: The tool does not run itself again every time the sheet is recalculated the way a built-in function does. Therefore, the analyst must rerun the HISTOGRAM tool if the data change.

Run the HISTOGRAM tool again. The panel will show the same entries, so this part will be quick. Check the plot option, run the tool, and then close. Edit the plot a little by changing the title, deleting the legend, and other things that seem favorable. To do these things, click on the item of interest to get a pop-up menu, then experiment. If you do not like what you see, use the UNDO feature to back up. UNDO is on the EDIT menu.

Data

Use this data set; it can also be found on the companion web site, www.ache.org/pubs/barry/start.cfm.

1.74	1.29	1.55	1.58	1.49
1.37	1.78	1.20	1.53	1.40
1.70	1.34	1.45	1.49	1.22
1.40	1.30	1.31	1.54	1.36
1.56	1.75	1.39	2.10	1.39
1.44	1.50	1.47	1.26	1.33

Analysis

If the process is undergoing normal fluctuations, 99.7 percent of the observations will fall within the process control limit band, by definition of the normal distribution. So, any point that falls outside the process control limits is a point to be studied further. It is not necessarily true that that point is wrong or that the process has suddenly gone out of control; rather, the point is so unusual that it invites close scrutiny.

Points that fall outside of the system limits occur only a few times in a million, so any point falling there is a cause for alarm. Something is wrong: sound the claxon.

In the case report, remark on any points that fall outside of the band. Mark any such points with an arrow or another highlight on the scatter diagram and on the histogram. If no points fall outside of the bands, remark to this effect in the report. To put a halo around a point on the chart, select the chart, select menu VIEW, and select TOOLBARS, which causes a submenu to appear. Select DRAWING. Drawing tools will appear across the bottom of the Excel® screen. Select the OVAL tool. Drag the mouse across the target data point and release. An oval will be drawn over the data point. The oval will probably be filled, which obscures the data point. To eliminate the fill, select the oval, right click to get the PROPERTIES menu, then select FORMAT AUTOSHAPE. Select the tab called COLORS AND LINES. Under the FILL section of the panel, drop down the list next to COLOR. At the top of the list is NO FILL; select this. Close the menu. The oval will now be a halo around the data point. Repeat the formatting process to set the oval's line to a suitable color. On the chart, select and drag the oval to position it suitably around the target data point.

Conclusion

The student will now have applied the basic tools, created a control chart with limits, observed aberrant points, and created a report for management.

CASE 2: PROCESS TRACKING

Topic: Process Observation and Analysis

The process control diagram created in Case 1 will be retained, and new data will be plotted on the same diagram. The new data will be observed to fall—or not fall—within the bands. Additional analysis will test the change in average value and standard deviation.

Work

1. Use the new data set below. Use the same process control limits and system limits that were found in Case 1. Do a scatter diagram.

   Observe that this data set seems to be off a little from the center of the bands. To see if this is within normal fluctuations, confidence intervals for the new and old data sets will be calculated.

2. Calculate the average and the standard deviation for the new data set. In addition, select a confidence level of 90 percent. Calculate the significance level by subtracting the confidence level from unity to get, in this case, 10 percent.

   Average value confidence interval: To calculate the confidence interval for the average value, calculate the Student's t factor for this data set, which has 30 data samples, by using the built-in function TINV(twice the significance factor, number of samples), in this case TINV(20%, 30). Multiply this by the standard deviation of the new data set. Add and subtract this from the set average value to get the confidence limits on the average value.

3. Repeat the step above using the average and standard deviation from Case 1. Compare the results.

4. Think of some way to plot the confidence intervals so that they can be compared directly by observation.

5. *Standard deviation confidence interval:* To set the confidence interval on the standard deviation with the same confidence factor and significance factor, calculate two factors using the chi-square distribution built-in functions.

   Lower multiplier: Calculate CHIINV[(significance level/2), sample count less one]. Using 90 percent confidence and 30 samples, that will be CHIINV(5%, 29). Divide the result into the sample-count-less-one, which in this case is 29. Take the square root of the result using SQRT(. . .); this gives the lower multiplier. Multiply the sample standard deviation by this to get the lower confidence limit on the standard deviation.

   Upper multiplier: Repeat this process for the upper limit, this time using CHIINV[(1 − significance level/2), sample count less one] or, in this case, CHIINV(95%, 29).

6. One way to compare samples is to compare the confidence intervals on their average values and standard deviations. Repeat the step above using the standard deviation for the data set from Case 1. Because the data sets are the same size, the multipliers are in fact the same.

7. Think of some way to plot the two sets of confidence intervals so that they can be compared directly by observation. Take care to distinguish the confidence intervals of the average from the confidence intervals of the standard deviation.

8. Note for future reference that the procedure above can be generalized by using the built-in function COUNT(. . .) to get the size of the sample set.

9. Include the scatter diagram and the confidence interval plots in the case report.

Data

Use this data set; it can also be found on the companion web site, www.ache.org/pubs/barry/start.cfm.

1.77	1.67	1.66	1.81	1.90
1.65	1.63	1.89	1.99	2.56
2.06	1.50	1.92	1.21	1.89
1.75	1.29	2.10	1.70	1.76
1.69	2.19	1.64	2.20	1.97
1.69	1.93	1.55	2.02	2.11

Analysis

Observe the scatter diagram. Remark on any special characteristics.

Observe the plots of the confidence intervals. If, when comparing the corresponding confidence intervals for the two data sets, you see substantial overlap, you have reason to believe the null hypothesis, which means that no change has taken place. On the other hand, if little or no overlap is seen, there is strong reason to believe that a change has occurred. If the confidence intervals overlap substantially, not enough information is in hand to make a crisp decision.

The confidence intervals will be smaller if a lower confidence level is used. (Try it and see!) Because the confidence intervals are smaller, the confidence intervals for two samples are less likely to overlap. What does that mean about the two samples?

Conclusion

The student will now be proficient in preparing and analyzing process tracking charts; he or she will have calculated confidence intervals for sample set averages and standard deviations.

CASE 3: PERFORMANCE EVALUATION

Topic: Six Sigma Limit Checks and Performance Ratios

In Case 1, system limits were calculated on the basis of the data set for that case. In Case 2, new data were gathered that appeared to show some drift and some change from Case 1. Now we will analyze this change and attempt to establish whether the change is significant.

If the underlying process has drifted away from its prior condition, the process may be in jeopardy of violating the system limits, so in this exercise we will check to see if the old system limits from Case 1 are still being respected. If not, new system limits will have to be issued, which will perturb the rest of the organization.

While we are at it, we will introduce two new statistical terms just so you will have seen them at least once.

Work

1. The companion web site, www.ache.org/pubs/barry/start.cfm, has the data from Cases 1 and 2 organized into one long column for Case 3. If you cannot access the web site at this time, copy the data from Cases 1 and 2 into one long column in a new spreadsheet.

   Copy the limit columns from Case 1, and extend the column entries so that the plot of the limit lines will look right. Do a scatter diagram of the combined data sets and the old limits.

2. We will now see if the average value has drifted more than 1.5 standard deviations away from its original value. Six Sigma allows for this much drift in the average value. This can be done in two ways. First, calculate the change in the average value between the

Case 1 data and the Case 2 data. Compare this change to 1.5 times the standard deviation from Case 1.

The present upper system limit is drawn six standard deviations above the average using the data from Case 1. Compare the average from Case 2 to the upper system limit minus 4.5 times the standard deviation from Case 1. Does this give the same result as the comparison just above? (Hint: It should!)

Include your conclusions in the case report. If you can figure out a graphical way to present the information, so much the better.

3. Traditional statistical process control has performance ratios that you should calculate once, just to become familiar with these terms. They are not needed elsewhere in this book, but they do appear in the literature from time to time.

The first is called the performance ratio, the symbol for which is C_p. This is defined as the system limit band divided by six times the sample standard deviation. For a well-behaved Six Sigma process, this ratio should be approximately 2.0. Calculate this for the sample set for Case 1 and again for the sample set for Case 2. Include the results in the case report.

4. The second traditional performance ratio is a proximity limit called $C_{p,k}$. Calculate the spacing between the sample average value and the closer system limit, then divide this by three times the sample standard deviation. For a well-behaving Six Sigma process, the ratio should be greater than 1.5.

Do this for the sample set for Case 1 and again for the sample data set for Case 2. Include the results in the case report.

Data

This case uses the data sets from Cases 1 and 2. These data are tabulated for Case 3 in the workbook found on the companion web site at www.ache.org/pubs/barry/start.cfm.

Analysis

If a substantial number of data sets were in hand, a new tracking chart could be made that would track the average sample set value. Such charts are often called X-bar charts, with X-bar meaning the average value for each sample set. What utility would such a tracking chart, which tracks average values, provide? What limit lines should a tracking chart for the average value use? Why? (Hint: What allowance is made in Six Sigma for drift in the average value?)

Suppose the tracking chart were not merely of the sample set average values but also of confidence intervals on the sample set average values, shown perhaps as bars on the tracking chart. What utility would such a tracking chart provide? What limits should this chart use? Why?

Include your remarks in the case report. (Hint: Six Sigma does not make any allowance for drift in the standard deviation.)

Conclusion

The student will now have mastery of scatter diagram manipulation and data tracking. He or she will also have applied the Six Sigma proximity limit analysis and the classic process performance ratio analysis.

CASE 4: POTENTIAL PROBLEM ANALYSIS

Topic: No-Stick Syringe Trial

This case applies potential problem analysis. For this exercise, we will consider a new technology, namely a certain type of no-stick syringe. The organization has become concerned by blood contamination and contagion possibilities that arise from traditional syringes that rely on administrative control to prevent inadvertent skin punctures. Vendors have proposed new syringe designs that have features that make needle sticks unlikely—but not impossible. These seem to be more cumbersome and perhaps more awkward to use because they have a surrounding structure encompassing the actual syringe, and they cost more, too. Still, needle sticks are a concern, and investigation of better devices is worthwhile.

Your organization has selected one product for trial. Your organization has not done any previous trial of new syringes, so there is no immediate basis for guessing what problems will arise in the trial. As project analyst, you will gather input and present a potential problem analysis. Your purpose is twofold. First, you must identify the potential problems. Second, you need to consider modifications to the trial plan to mitigate some of the potential problems.

Work

1. Create a potential problem analysis diagram. Identify at least four kinds of potential problems. Make a bulleted list of concerns for each kind of potential problem.
2. Improve the analysis by gathering input from others. If that is not workable, put yourself in the role of purchasing agent and think about the issues from the purchasing agent's perspective. Repeat in the role of the patient care unit nurse, the emergency nurse, the surgeon, and so on.
3. Propose at least one change to the trial to mitigate one or more of the potential problems.
4. Include the potential problem analysis diagram in the case report.
5. Include at least one bulleted list of details for each of the types of problems.
6. Include the recommended trial change in the case report.

Data

No data are required for this case.

Analysis

What level of detail should the potential problem analysis include? What parties are included in the development of the potential problem analysis? What should the analyst do if a potential problem comes to light that is so great as to cast the project in doubt?

Conclusion

The student will have considered the potential problems arising from a typical technology change in a healthcare organization, gathered input from others, and recommended an improvement in the trial of the new technology to mitigate a potential problem.

CASE 5: YIELD

Topic: Cumulative Process Performance

In this exercise, you will calculate results over several stages of service. The goal of the organization is to make sure everything is done right the first time. Expressed quantitatively, this is called the first-time-through yield.

When errors are few, counting errors is easier than counting successes. The error rate is the error count divided by the total number of opportunities for error. Yield is then defined as the complement of the error rate (the error rate subtracted from one); an error rate of 0.1 percent means a yield of 99.9 percent.

This can be seen by counting lost units. Suppose we start with 10,000 units and two process steps, each of which has an error rate of 0.1 percent and, therefore, a yield of 99.9 percent. The first process step loses 0.1 percent of 10,000 units, which is equal to 10 units. The second step loses 0.1 percent of 9,990 units, which is 9.99 units. The total loss is 19.99 units; we will call it 20. So, the overall yield is 10,000 minus the losses, in this case, 9,980. As a fraction of the starting quantity, the yield is 99.8 percent.

For low error rates, the error rates for several stages can be added together without appreciable loss of precision in the result. For example, in the two-step case above, the difference between a precise calculation and simply adding up the per-stage error rate is the difference between 19.99 and 20.00; this is negligible.

If there are five stages and the overall error rate goal is 3.4 per million, the error rate per stage must average only one-fifth of 3.4 per million, or about 0.7 per million. If there are ten stages of service, the per-stage error rate must be all the smaller at 0.34 per million.

When selecting projects for improvement, the eye is drawn to those stages of service that contribute most of the total error. For any such improvement, the goal should be to get the error rate for that stage down to its proper share of the organization error rate allowance or better.

Work

1. An organization finds that its accounting system enters into the service process many times. The accounting system error rate is 25 errors per million transactions, and there are 200 accounting transactions in the typical patient's record. What is the number of accounting errors to be expected in one patient's account? (Hint: Multiply the error rate by the number of opportunities for

error. Remember to divide by one million, because the error rate is given per million. The result is the expected number of errors per patient.)

2. Considering the rest of the treatment as one lumped-together stage with an error rate of seven per million opportunities, and estimating that there are an average of 500 opportunities for error in the average patient's treatment, what is the number of treatment errors to be expected in one patient's treatment?

3. What is the composite error rate, considering both accounting and treatment? (Hint: Add together the two error results from above, noting that both are stated as expected errors per patient. This sum will be the composite expected errors per patient.)

4. What is the likelihood that any one patient will have neither an accounting error nor a treatment error? (Hint: Try one minus the likelihood of having one error or the other.) This is the first-time-through yield. (We ignore the effect of any one patient's account having more than one error, because the error rate is small. The complete calculation is shown in the appendix.)

5. Standard deviations are determined like the sides of a triangle: by adding their squares and taking the square root of the sum. Suppose the standard deviation of the two kinds of error is two errors per million accounting transactions and three errors per million treatment opportunities. What is the standard deviation of the composite for any patient? (Hint: Multiply these per-unit values times the number of transactions of each type to get values per patient, then add the squares and take the square root.)

6. Using these results, and considering a sample of 1,000 patients, what is the number of patients expected to have no accounting errors and no treatment errors? (Hint: Multiply the first-time-through yield by the population being considered.) What is the standard deviation of this number? (Hint: Do the same with the standard deviation.)

7. State the Six Sigma system limits that apply to the overall service process. (Hint: Remember that the system limits are six standard deviations away from the average and that in this case the average is the first-time-through yield. If the upper system limit exceeds 100 percent, set it at 100 percent, as a yield above 100 percent is physically impossible.)

Data

No additional data are required for this case. The companion web site, www.ache.org/pubs/barry/start.cfm, has a worksheet that may be helpful in carrying out the analysis.

Analysis

The goal is to drive the error rate down below 3.4 per million; however, it may not be within the capability of the present system to meet the goal. The system limits are a conservative statement of what the present system can do. If the system is improved, the system limits can be tightened, but it is not rational to expect the present system to do better than what the system limits portray.

Does the first-time-through yield fall within the system limits? If the accounting transaction rate were reduced by a factor of ten, would that make an appreciable difference in the overall system performance? Estimate one or two pairs of error rates that would give an overall yield of 99.9997 percent because that would demonstrate Six Sigma performance.

Conclusion

The student will have computed the yield for a two-stage service process and can readily extend this to any number of stages. He or she will have reflected on the difference between the goal of 3.4 errors per million and the capability of the present system as characterized by the system limits.

CASE 6: TEST RELIABILITY

Topic: Interpreting Measured Values

In this exercise, we will apply two-stage yield analysis to testing. Instruments can give the right output, but they can also give a false-positive or a false-negative output. This is of greatest concern when an instrument is set to monitor a condition and to activate an alarm or warning when a measured parameter violates a range limit. Both false conditions are worrisome because a false-negative condition means that the alarm function is defeated, and a false-positive condition means that confidence in the alarm system will wane.

If the instrument is monitoring an important process directly, such as the patient's temperature, the error rate is simply that of the instrument itself. If the instrument is monitoring a machine that is performing a function, and if both the machine and the instrument are subject to error, analysis needs to take into consideration the error rates of both the machine and the instrument.

Suppose the machine is a tester that looks at blood samples and declares whether or not the blood is type O+ and then produces two streams, one of declared O+ and the other of declared *not* O+. The machine can make two types of error: one is the false-positive error of declaring a sample to be O+ when in fact it is not; the other is the false-negative error of declaring a sample not to be O+ when in fact it is.

Because the point of the machine is to produce a stream of samples that the machine thinks are O+, we will pay attention to that stream and ignore the other stream of samples that the machine thinks are not O+. We will call the former the machine-selected stream, and we will not talk about the other stream at all.

The machine-selected stream will contain some number of samples that should not be there because in fact the machine made an error in letting them in. We will call this the machine's error rate, which is also the false-positive error rate.

Because this is an important matter, we will test this machine-selected stream with a tester. The tester does the same sort of examination again, testing whether the samples in this stream are indeed O+ in the tester's opinion. What we want this tester to be particularly good at is picking out samples that are not in fact O+ and rejecting them. If it rejects some good O+ samples, too, that is unfortunate, but it is tolerable.

We will divide the machine-selected stream into two fictional streams, one of true O+ samples and one of false O+ samples, so that we can consider how the tester treats each kind of sample. The tester will have a distinct error rate for each kind of sample, so it is convenient to pretend there are two samples, each entirely composed of good O+ or bad O+ samples. With this leap of imagination, we can draw a little diagram.

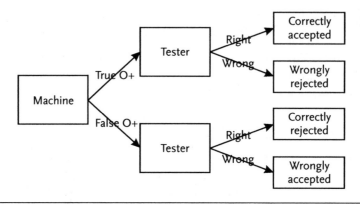

The matter of greatest concern is the sample that is not O+ that goes through the tester, the tester makes a false-positive finding, and the sample is accepted as if it were an O+ sample. The final output stream will consist of these hopefully few not-O+ samples plus the true O+ samples. The tester will also falsely reject some number of true O+ samples by making a false-negative finding.

Let us use some error-rate parameters for the tester and see what the outcomes are.

Blood Sample Tester

Stream Contains	False-Positive Rate	False-Negative Rate
True O+ samples		Five per 1,000
False O+ samples	Three per 1,000	

Suppose that the original machine had a false-positive rate of eight per 1,000. Now we have a two-stage process, and we have all the parameters necessary to calculate the makeup of the output stream that is supposed to contain almost entirely true O+ samples. Of those samples identified as O+ after the test and the check, how many are really O+? Because the error rate of the checking instrument appears to be worse than the error rate of the machine, one may suspect that the checking may do more harm than good.

The work below involves a lot of opportunities for getting the wrong factor in the wrong place. The safe way to proceed is to draw a little diagram. On the left, show the tester with two output streams: one correct and one false. Connect the "correct" line to a checker box, which itself has two outputs: true positive and false negative. Connect the "false" line to a separate checker box, which itself has two outputs: true negative and false positive. Write the fractions next to each line. Write the calculated values on the diagram as they are produced so that you can keep track of the results.

Work

1. Using the machine false-positive error rate and the tester false-positive rate, calculate the composite error rate. (Hint: Refer to Case 5.) This is the impurity rate in the final O+ stream.
2. Calculate the machine's yield, which is 100 percent minus the false-positive error rate. Use this value and the tester's false-negative rate to calculate the fraction of the stream that is falsely rejected by the tester.
3. Refer to the diagram above, which shows the tester with two input streams and four output streams. In the previous two steps, you have calculated the stream fractions for two of the four output streams. Now calculate the other two so that all of the input flow will be accounted for in the output flows.
4. Include a diagram in your report. On the diagram, enter the output stream fractions.

Data

The error rates for the machine and the tester are given above.

Analysis

What is the purity of the final stream of O+ samples? How does this compare with the purity rate of the samples coming out of the machine? Does the tester improve the purity of the output stream? If so, what is the reduction in the impurity achieved by the tester stage?

Suppose it is physically possible to add a second tester downstream of the present tester, and suppose that the error rates of the second tester are the same as those of the present tester. How much further improvement, if any, would you expect to be achieved by an added stage of testing?

At each stage of testing, some of the product is lost to false negatives. How would you trade off additional purity achieved by additional testing against loss of product to false negatives?

Conclusion

The student will have observed by now that, although the arithmetic in this kind of analysis is not very complicated, the opportunity for confusion is great. Drawing a diagram is good practice.

The student will have analyzed a complex two-stage process and computed the effective yield of this process. He or she will have seen that the practice of drawing out processes in simple diagrams is rewarding because it clarifies thinking and captures that thinking in a useful way. More complex systems can be analyzed in this way, provided a suitable diagram can be drawn.

CASE 7: TIME-VALUE CHARTS

Topic: Comparing Two Scenarios

Time-value charts are helpful tools for the analysis of multistep problems, especially those that involve delays of various kinds. Draw a line, starting at the left side of the page, and move the pencil to the right to represent a period of time. If no value is being added at the time, the line runs horizontally. If some value is being added, the line rises on a slope so that the rise is proportional to the value added. Precision in time is usually more important than precision in value.

For this example, consider that a certain medical book is to be ordered online or purchased at the nearest university bookstore. Suppose that the price will be about the same either way.

Work

1. Draw a time-value line for the online purchase scenario.
2. Draw a second time-value line for the trip to the university bookstore.
3. Include both lines in the project report.
4. Repeat the work above, this time considering the matter from the point of view of your organization, and consider the fact that time

spent by you away from your station is a negative value to your organization. Buying the book, however, is a positive value to your organization.

Data

No additional data are required for this case.

Analysis

Consider which of the strategies is better from each of the two points of view; include any other observations.

This technique is useful for the analysis of multistep processes from the view of the patient and from the view of the healthcare organization. Indeed, there may be several different points of view in practical situations. The sketch can bring these points of view to light and, perhaps, aid in reconciling conflicting interests.

Conclusion

The student will have analyzed time-value sketches from two points of view and used these as simple devices to explain a multistep process.

CASE 8: THE POISSON DISTRIBUTION

Topic: Discrete Events Modeling

The normal distribution gets the most use, but other distributions are of practical interest as well. This case considers the Poisson distribution, which applies to discrete events, each of low probability. Experience shows that the Poisson distribution applies to the number of telephone calls attempted during a busy hour, the number of patrons showing up at a bank branch during the lunch hour, the number of people showing up to use an automatic teller machine at mid-afternoon on Friday, and so on.

These scenarios are important because service organizations cannot possibly design themselves to serve their clients if every one of the clients shows up at once. A bank may have 10,000 depositors, and if all of them show up at once, the bank is going to be swamped. In addition, the bank cannot possibly build a building big enough to take care of a surge of 10,000 customers. Because 100 percent capacity is not going to be provided, what should be the basis for some reasonable level of capacity?

The immediate follow-up question is, what is to be done if a surge in demand exceeds the service capacity provided? If these surges are sufficiently rare, the organization can plead that all reasonable measures were already taken. If the surges are not sufficiently rare, the client population may look elsewhere for service.

The Poisson distribution also applies to trial evaluations when errors are of low probability. If the expected number of errors per 1,000 events is three, what should be considered if the observed error rate is zero? Or four?

The Poisson distribution has one odd feature: the standard deviation and the average are not independent of each other the way they are in the normal distribution. Instead, the standard deviation is the square root of the average value for the Poisson distribution.

The Poisson distribution does not have the bell-curve profile seen in common applications; rather, it has a steeper slope on the left-hand side and a less steep slope on the right-hand side. The curve stops at the origin because a negative number of discrete events has no meaning. The Poisson distribution does take on the familiar bell shape if the average is a large number, but that is not the range of interest or purpose when the Poisson distribution is being applied.

Sometimes it is of interest to check the distribution to find out how likely it is that a particular number of events should occur. More often, there is a range of numbers of interest given the question, "What range of occurrences might one expect with 95 percent confidence?" With that answer, the organization can establish a capacity to deal with 95 percent of the occurrences and have a defendable position. The 95 percent value is a confidence level; if the organization has the matching capacity, the organization, with 95 percent confidence, can handle the traffic. The 95 percent value is also called a "service level" when it is used to size capacity.

For this case, consider an emergency room located near a metal-working factory that employs 2,000 workers and where workers get burned badly enough to require care 12 times a month, on average. The number varies from month to month and seems to follow a Poisson distribution, as indeed it should if the burns result from random accidents in the course of work. The maximum number of cases might be 2,000, if every worker got burned. To provide capacity to treat 2,000 cases would seem to be rash, given that the average number is only 12. What is a reasonable number of cases to use as the planning basis?

Work

1. Open a spreadsheet and create a column of numbers running from 0 to 25. In the adjacent column, enter the Poisson distribution values, or ordinates, for the average value of 12. In the next column, do the same, but enter the cumulative Poisson distribution for each of the numbers in the first column. In Excel®, the Poisson function is POISSON(x, mean, cumulative?). The x value is the number in the first column, the mean is the average value, namely 12, and the third argument is "false" for the ordinate column and "true" for the cumulative column. The cumulative column sums up all of the values from zero up to the present number. (Hint: Be sure to start counting from zero, not from one.)
2. Create a chart of the ordinate column, which will look a little like a bell curve but will not be symmetric.
3. Create a chart of the third column, which will be an S-curve rising to near unity.
4. Include both charts in the report.
5. What is the likelihood of having exactly ten burns in a month? (Hint: Read the ordinate column.)
6. What fraction of the total possibilities will be ten or fewer cases in a month? (Hint: Read the cumulative column.)
7. What number is so large that 95 percent of all possibilities will be that number or less? (Hint: Work backward from the cumulative column.) What about for 90 percent?

Data

The primary datum needed for this exercise is that the average value is 12.

Analysis

Experiment with different average values; try 4, and try 25. You will see that the distribution is quite skewed for the average value of 4 and much like a bell curve for 25. For large average values, not much distinction is seen between the normal curve and the Poisson curve, so it is not rash to take advantage of the convenience of using the normal curve in many cases, even where the Poisson curve might be better justified from a theoretical basis.

Excel® does not provide an inverse Poisson function, so it is necessary to generate the list of cumulative values to get the argument corresponding to, say, 95 percent.

In your report, recommend a service level, and recommend the matching capacity requirement for burn treatments starting with the average case rate of 12 per month. Defend your recommendations.

Conclusion

The student will have analyzed a discrete event of low probability using the Poisson distribution, which is useful in sizing capacities to serve large populations, not all of whom are expected to need the service at the same time. He or she will also have applied a service level to establish the capacity plan.

CASE 9: INCOMPLETE TRIALS

Topic: Cumulative Analysis

In this exercise, we will dealing with incomplete trials by analyzing cumulative data. A trial often produces incomplete information. For instance, if 20 people join a trial and 4 of them are reassigned during the trial and therefore do not complete their part, 20 percent of the potential data are not going to be available. Although this can be dealt with by accepting a reduced data set or starting with extra participants to allow for some shrinkage, it is helpful to have some technique for dealing with the incomplete data in a systematic way. There is such a technique for duration testing, which is also called life testing.

Start with a population of samples to be tested for lifetime. For those that reach the end state, collect the data. For those that do not reach the end state, note the time at which they dropped out of the test.

Sort the data so that the longest-lived is first and the shortest-lived is last, including the dropouts. Highlight the dropouts to distinguish them from the others.

Count the data points. Note the top 10 percent, the top 20 percent, and so on through the top 90 percent. For example, if there were 50 items at the start and 10 dropped out, the top 10 percent is the top 5.

A reasonable confidence interval on the lifetime can then be read directly from these results, with the 90 percent confidence interval corresponding to the top 90 percent result. This is necessarily conservative because the dropouts could not have had a shorter lifetime than their dropout time.

If the population is large, the confidence intervals can be improved somewhat by fitting the data to the cumulative distribution of the most likely model, such as a bathtub curve. If the population has 20 or fewer members, the uncertainty in the fit outweighs any gain from the modeling.

Consider this scenario. A trial gets underway to test the value, utility, and user satisfaction of pocket-sized computers for use by orderlies in a long-term-care facility. As the analyst, you note that a potential problem is battery lifetime. No information is available that would help you gauge lifetime, yet you need some estimate of lifetime so that you can plan for replacement units when, if the trial is successful, the computers are issued to all employees. So, you arrange to collect data on battery lifetime as an adjunct to the trial.

During the trial, various things happen. Some computers get damaged and are dropped out of the trial. Two of the people using the computers in the trial are transferred to other assignments, and they turn in their computers. At the end of the trial, you need to extract such information so that you can pull together the data gathered on battery life.

Work

1. Enter the data given below into a spreadsheet, and note that the data are already available in computer format on the companion web site, www.ache.org/pubs/barry/start.cfm. Sort the data in descending order. To do this, select menu DATA, select SORT, then select DESCENDING, and pick the data set for sorting.
2. Move those data that are marked "incomplete" to a second column so that, when the data are plotted, these will get a different ink color. Drag and drop, using the mouse. Plot the data using horizontal bars.

3. Count off the top 10 percent, 20 percent, 50 percent, 75 percent, and 90 percent.
4. Report the 75 percent confidence lifetime (the cutoff for the top 75 percent of lifetimes). On the basis of this trial, 75 percent or more of computers put into use can expect to have a battery lifetime at least this long.

Data

ID	Life	Event	ID	Life	Event
A	24.0	OK	K	27.0	OK
B	10.0	OK	L	21.5	OK
C	16.5	OK	M	11.0	OK
D	20.0	Broken	N	28.0	OK
E	25.5	OK	O	19.5	Broken
F	28.5	OK	P	19.0	OK
G	18.5	OK	Q	17.6	OK
H	16.0	OK	R	19.0	OK
I	13.0	Quit	S	18.0	OK
J	17.5	Quit	T	19.0	OK

The lifetime is quoted in days. The event is marked "OK" if the event was a normal battery replacement. These data can also be found on the companion web site, www.ache.org/pubs/barry/start.cfm.

Analysis

Consider what would happen to this analysis if half of the participants dropped out after five days. (Hint: What would happen to the 75 percent cutoff?) Consider what would happen if the not-OK items were simply deleted from the study. Would the 75 percent cutoff go up or down? Note that no assumption is made in this analysis about the nature of the distribution function governing battery lifetime. The procedure simply ranks the outcomes without trying to find any parameters for functions.

Like all statistical methods of analysis, this procedure is weak if the data sample set is small. Even so, if only a few data samples are available, this procedure is better than nothing, and it makes productive use of even the defective data samples.

Conclusion

The student will have analyzed lifetime data samples, including defective samples, to estimate confidence intervals for studies of lifetimes.

CASE 10: FAILURE MODES AND EFFECTS

Topic: Linkages

Failures happen. The systematic analysis of failures is necessary to prevent recurrence. This book has dealt with chains of events, fishbone diagrams, and failure modes and effects analysis. All of these are useful, and all seek to portray the linkages between actions, events, and consequences. Of these, failure modes and effects analysis deals directly with failure analysis. Something failed. Something might fail. What happens then?

A failure modes and effects analysis can be done to any depth. For example, say that a part broke. What things might have caused the part to break? Of these things, what might have caused them? These linkages can be drawn out in an ever-expanding tree. Proceeding in the other direction, if the part fails, what happens then? And if that happens, what happens as a consequence? Again, you can build another ever-expanding tree. Generally it is useful to carry out failure modes and effects analysis for at least two steps in each direction. The nature of the particular event will then dictate whether further expansion would be helpful.

In drawing out the tree, it is customary to reserve judgment as to which is the most likely until the tree is drawn out sufficiently. At that point, judgment and experience can usually narrow down the branches of interest, with the others held in reserve.

In this case, suppose that the healthcare organization provides bed care for patients and that, in recent months, three patients have fallen out of bed during the nighttime hours. Each bed has rails, each patient has access to a call-button with an attendant on call, and there is a stepstool beside each bed. In short, the system had been designed to prevent the very falls that are now being observed.

Because more than one patient is involved, there must be a system problem. Linking relationships between the effect (a fallen patient) and the possible causes (the failure[s] of the prevention devices) may be illuminating.

Work

1. Draw a failure modes and effects tree to portray the linkage between the prevention devices and the event. Carry the tree out to three or four stages. Use separate sheets as necessary for legibility. Include the tree or trees in the report.
2. Identify the two or three most likely problems, using your own judgment. Form a hypothesis as to the most likely cause. Include the hypothesis in the report.
3. Identify additional data that would be required to validate the hypothesis. Include the data list in the report, perhaps in summary form.
4. Identify a test or trial program that would provide the validation data. Include recommendations in the report.

Data

No additional data are required for this case.

Analysis

The most common benefit of such analysis is to organize the thinking of a work group to forestall any jumping to conclusions. For this reason alone, a failure modes and effects analysis is often worthwhile.

In situations like the one in this case, it is commonly found that the preventive measures the system provided would have worked but that they were defeated by the patient, a visitor, or staff. Designing preventive measures that cannot be defeated is an ongoing challenge. Monitoring systems (bed rail up?) and alarms are an interesting design problem, and perhaps a good solution will arise that will provide a practicable solution.

Conclusion

The student will have applied failure modes and effects analysis to a practical problem.

CASE 11: DISCRETE ANALYSIS

Topic: Known Populations

In some cases, the total population of interest is known and can be counted. If so, specific methods apply. Consider the following case. The organization has a number of gurneys for moving patients around the building. The gurneys are to be returned to the gurney pool at the end of each use, and some data gathering shows that any one gurney is at the pool location 40 percent of the time. The organization has considered how many gurneys need to be on hand in the pool at any time, and the organization has established a policy that, with 90 percent confidence, at least seven gurneys will be at the pool location to take care of surges in demand.

The department manager identifies two possible approaches. One is to hire a gurney wrangler to walk the floors and bring back orphaned gurneys the way grocery stores hire shopping cart wranglers to round up shopping carts in parking lots. The second option is to buy more gurneys, if the right number to buy can be determined.

For a fixed population of gurneys, the likelihood that at least seven will be in the pool can be calculated using the binomial distribution. The binomial distribution applies when exactly two states are possible: in this case, the gurney is either in the pool or it is not. Thus, the binomial distribution applies. (If there were three or more possibilities, another distribution, the multinomial, would apply.) The binomial distribution requires the following input: the target count, the total population count, and the probability. If the total population of gurneys were 12 and the probability 40 percent, the confidence level for finding *at least* seven gurneys in the pool would be the sum of the likelihoods of finding 7, 8, 9, 10, 11, or 12 gurneys in the pool.

The likelihood of *not* finding at least seven gurneys in the pool would be the sum of the likelihoods of finding zero, one, two, three, four, five, or six in the pool. The sum of the two likelihoods (finding and not finding at least seven gurneys in the pool) must be 100 percent. The binomial distribution looks like the normal distribution for most sets of parameters. It is available as a built-in function in Excel® and in other spreadsheet applications.

Work

1. Open a spreadsheet. Create a column of numbers running from 0 to 12. (Hint: Be sure to include 0.) Label this the "Count" column; this corresponds to the number of gurneys in the pool at any one time.

In the next column, compute the corresponding binomial distribution values given a total population of 12 and a probability of 40 percent. Use BINOMDIST(count, population size, probability, false). The "false" entry tells the function to return the distribution value or ordinate rather than the cumulative distribution.

Plot the distribution.

2. In a third column, compute for each count in the first column the cumulative binomial distribution by using BINOMDIST(count, population size, true). Plot these values.

3. Returning to the question of how many gurneys should be in the population to have at least seven in the pool given that the probability of any one gurney being in the pool is 40 percent, note that BINOMDIST(6, 17, 40%, true) would return likelihood of six or fewer gurneys being in the pool if the total population is 17. Because what is wanted is not that but rather the opposite, the desired result will be returned by calculating one minus BINOMDIST(6, 17, 40%, true).

Create a column of population sizes running from 12 to 40. Fill in the next column using the values found for one minus BINOMDIST(6, population size, probability, true). This column is, for each population size, the likelihood of having seven or more gurneys in the pool. Plot these points.

4. From the above, select the population size that would give 90 percent confidence that at least seven gurneys will be in the pool. Include this in the report.

Data

No additional data are required for this case.

Analysis

How much would the confidence level improve if five additional gurneys were acquired? How much would the confidence level fall if five fewer gurneys were acquired?

In analyzing the potential problems that might arise if this policy is followed, the analyst considers that people might be less diligent in returning gurneys to the pool if more of them are in the total population. Suppose the in-pool probability drops to 35 percent. How much would the confidence level drop? How many more gurneys would be needed to make up for the drop in in-pool probability? Consider these matters for inclusion in the report.

Conclusion

The student will have performed a service improvement analysis using discrete analysis. He or she will have considered the importance of incremental changes in the population size and in the probability parameter.

CASE 12: CENTRAL LIMIT THEOREM

Topic: Central Tendency

Nature sides with the bell-shaped curve. The normal distribution is used in statistical analysis both for convenience and to take advantage of a powerful central tendency captured in the central limit theorem. This theorem states that estimates of the average value will be distributed by the normal distribution with the same average value as that of the underlying population and that the standard deviation of the sample average will be equal to the standard deviation of the underlying population divided by the square root of the sample size as the total number of samples grows to a large number.

So, if the underlying population is, say, Poisson, the distribution of samples averages from this distribution will be the normal distribution. If the underlying population is binomial, the distribution of sample averages from this distribution will be the normal distribution. The same is true for any underlying population. (The theorem requires the standard deviation of the underlying population be finite, which is always true in real situations.)

The standard deviation of the sample average will go to zero as the sample size grows, so the sample average will be known more and more precisely as the sample size grows. This theorem applies even if the sample average being tracked is the sum of samples drawn from various distributions.

The practical effect of this remarkable theorem is that any sample average can be modeled using the normal distribution. Because almost any parameter being observed is the result of several subprocesses acting to give an accumulated result, that observed parameter is going to behave according to the normal distribution. Thus it is a reasonable practice in the real world to presume that the normal distribution applies unless a clear indication exists to think otherwise.

This case will demonstrate the central limit theorem by drawing samples from the uniform distribution, which is handily available in Excel® as a built-in function. The uniform distribution returns a result which is between 0 and 1, with all numbers in between being equally likely. This is not a bell curve; it is a flat line. The Excel® function is RAND(). Other spreadsheet applications use similar but different names. RAND() is a volatile function, so every time the sheet is recalculated, the value returned by RAND() changes. Test this by hitting the F9 key, which forces a recalculation of the page. Repeat this several times.

To freeze the value, do the following. Select the cells to be frozen. Select menu EDIT, then select COPY. Close the menu. Select EDIT, select PASTE SPECIAL, and then select VALUES on the panel. Close the menu. This writes the values into the same cells in which RAND() had been located. This process is destructive, so if you want to generate the RAND() results again, it is necessary to type the RAND() formulae in again. An in-between approach is to copy the frozen values onto a different sheet so that the formulae are preserved.

Work

1. Open a spreadsheet. Make a column of 20 entries, all of them being equal to RAND(). Note that the cells all have different values, even though the cell formulae are all the same. Hit F9 a few times to cause the sheet to be recalculated. Note that the values in the column are volatile.

   Freeze the values. Copy the values onto a new spreadsheet or onto a blank part of the same spreadsheet, using the PASTE SPECIAL/ VALUES procedure given above. Create a histogram of these frozen values using a small bin size. (Refer back to Cases 1, 2, and 3 to refresh your memory regarding bins and histograms.) Plot the histogram. Remark in the report whether this distribution appears to be more or less uniform.

2. Return to the sheet with the column of random numbers. Copy the column several times so that the sheet will have 50 columns of 20 rows, all being samples from the uniform distribution. Calculate

the average and standard deviation for the whole set of 1,000 cells. Report your results.

3. For each of the 20 columns, compute the average. Make a histogram of these set averages. Plot the results. Note for the report whether the distribution of these set averages appears to be uniform, bell-shaped, or other. (Hint: The central limit theorem suggests that the distribution will be the normal distribution.)

4. Force recalculation of the sheet by hitting F9 a few times. Note whether the plot of averages changes with each recalculation. Note whether the histogram of averages changes. (Hint: The histogram does not update itself automatically. To force an update, use the TOOLS menu/DATA ANALYSIS/ HISTOGRAM.) Report your findings.

Data

No additional data are required for this case.

Analysis

Before computers were on every desk, random numbers were published in large books. Books of normally distributed random numbers were generated by adding up seven random numbers drawn from the uniform distribution, which was a direct application of the central limit theorem. All cumulative distributions are uniform between zero and unity, by definition. Therefore, it is possible to create a random number generator for any distribution for which an inverse function is at hand. For example, Excel® provides an inverse function for the normal distribution, so a normally distributed random number generator can be written by the formula =NORMINV(RAND(), AVERAGE, STANDARD DEVIATION) for any specified average value and standard deviation. Try a column of these with average value of zero and standard deviation of one. The cells will all have the formula =NORMINV(RAND(),0,1). Hit F9 a few times to force a recalculation so you can see the dynamic. Create and plot a histogram. Does this look like a normal distribution?

Conclusion

The student will have demonstrated the validity of the central limit theorem by manipulating random numbers from the uniform distribution.

He or she will have generated normally distributed random numbers in two ways: by the direct application of the central limit theorem and by combining built-in spreadsheet functions.

CASE 13: DATA SAMPLING

Topic: Reduced Tracking Methods

One way to reduce effort is by sampling the data. Analysis of a partial data set, a sample, works fine if the sample is a high-fidelity representation of the underlying population. If a lot of data are available to start with, as might be the case when analyzing past data that happens to be at hand, random sampling can be used. Suppose there are 100 patient records, and you want to look at 10 of them. Open a spreadsheet, make a column that goes from 1 to 100, make a second column of random numbers, freeze the random numbers, and then sort the table in order of descending random numbers. Take the case numbers from the top ten rows of the sorted table. You now have ten randomly selected cases.

For ongoing projects, it is usually difficult to organize activities so that data are taken at random. Taking temperatures at the end of a shift is not done at random; taking temperatures after meals is not done at random. Either of these processes may be fine for other purposes, but they are not random samples of a patient's temperature over the entirety of the day. Alternatively, it is not likely to be rewarding to wake a patient up at three o'clock in the morning to get a temperature sample just to conform to a random-interval sampling plan.

Practicable data sampling for ongoing projects is likely to be periodic: once a shift, once a day, or once every hour. For this example, we will look at the once-an-hour sampling plan. If the underlying process has a component that also varies slowly, this may be a good periodic sampling plan. On the other hand, if the underlying process varies rapidly or has brief episodes, this plan will miss important features of the data. A good understanding of the process being sampled is necessary.

How should you proceed? Past experience is an excellent guide. However, if no past experience is available, start sampling frequently, observe the data, and extend the sampling period gradually.

The act of sampling presents opportunities for error in reading and transcribing the sample values. To the extent that these are random, they do not matter much unless the data set is very small. If they are not random because, say, a gauge is read from an angle to one side so that the readings always err on the low side, a bias introduces itself into the process. If estimation is required, the reading error can be quite substantial. For example, an estimate of a patient's weight is not likely to be very precise.

Work

1. Organize the data set below into one long column on a spreadsheet; it can also be found on the companion web site, www.ache.org/ pubs/barry/start.cfm. Compute the average value and the standard deviation. Create a histogram with some reasonable bin size to visualize the data. Select some information for the report.
2. Try a periodic sampling plan, say every tenth row, and make a new column with this sample set. [One way to have the spreadsheet do this is to create a counter column that gives the row number. Set the sample spacing in a cell. In the sample data column, write a formula such as =IF(MOD(counter, spacing)=0, neighboring value from full set, 0).] Compute the parameters of the sample set. Compute the 90 percent confidence intervals on the sample average and sample standard deviation. Do a TTEST(. . .) and an FTEST(. . .) to compare the sample set and the original set. Do a histogram. Form an opinion on the goodness of the fit of the sampling plan.
3. Repeat with some other sampling plans. Select one or two parameters as good measures of the sampling plans and plot these. Include the plot in the report.
4. Select a sampling plan to recommend to management.

Data

This is the full data set, from which reduced samples are to be drawn; it can also be found on the companion web site.

Full Data Set

14.34	16.46	12.23	19.17	17.41
17.60	12.39	16.71	16.78	15.57
13.30	13.48	17.12	13.88	18.07

(continued on following page)

(Continued)

Full Data Set

16.24	16.86	15.51	18.10	18.30
15.09	9.14	18.73	18.83	13.41
17.59	19.49	16.29	15.23	15.18
15.23	16.94	13.61	17.80	18.50
18.01	14.85	14.47	17.10	18.95
13.71	14.93	20.91	17.19	16.23
12.98	20.70	16.05	17.56	19.79
17.67	13.54	15.78	17.34	12.29
13.48	15.69	19.16	13.12	17.30
17.04	19.60	15.81	15.98	19.22
19.35	17.34	14.60	19.52	12.73
10.21	16.73	19.89	13.65	16.35
15.82	18.35	14.51	15.28	19.13
17.01	14.69	14.44	18.74	15.12
17.12	13.36	19.28	11.37	14.61
16.40	17.87	18.47	14.63	18.82
19.43	15.08	13.91	20.19	15.99
17.11	14.00	15.01	14.87	18.30
14.22	14.88	16.19	17.84	15.45
18.71	17.97	16.52	16.53	11.92
15.84	15.13	18.20	16.69	14.13
15.23	15.25	16.35	15.74	16.40
19.91	16.22	17.38	19.91	13.20
16.32	14.91	18.11	15.27	17.07
18.66	17.14	13.54	14.22	18.83
16.37	14.24	16.84	17.90	15.96
17.46	19.54	15.97	17.54	12.77
18.65	20.80	15.94	18.34	20.48
16.97	14.12	14.90	18.83	14.05
17.83	12.85	17.23	13.02	17.77
15.54	15.63	15.93	16.68	17.11
18.14	14.28	16.74	18.01	14.27
15.75	15.05	18.32	15.86	14.68
17.20	14.69	16.81	20.07	21.54
14.80	17.05	15.10	16.32	14.75
16.57	15.56	20.22	15.61	11.90
14.85	17.49	11.86	15.70	18.41

Analysis

If taking more samples costs more time and effort in a linear way so that taking twice as many samples takes twice as much effort, is there a best choice for the sampling plan? How would you address this issue? What visualizations of the original data set and any sample set give the most insight into the goodness of fit of the sample plan?

Any sampling plan would have to be run on a trial basis to confirm that it works in practice as well as it works on the blackboard. State your method for deciding how long to run such a trial.

Include these findings in your report.

Conclusion

The student will have considered random sampling to reduce data acquisition cost by testing candidate sampling plans against a full data set. He or she will have considered classical analysis of the sample sets and visualization of the results and will have considered the minimum running time for a trial to validate the selected sampling plan.

CASE 14: RULE-BASED SAMPLING

Topic: Focused Tracking Methods

It may be helpful to create a rule for when samples are to be taken. Rule-based sampling focuses attention on key times and key events, which are times when random sampling or periodic sampling would not provide sufficient insight.

When a machine is turned on, the obvious thing to do is to check it and its setup immediately to see if it is operable. Electronics are known to fail most often just when the machine is turned on, so the fact that the machine ran yesterday is not sufficient to know that it will run today. Indeed, most computerized machines check themselves upon boot-up for this very reason.

A computer self-check is limited to the computer and its slaved equipment, so a computer self-check is usually not a sufficient test of the equipment. It is necessary to verify that leads are connected properly, that any supplies are loaded in, and so on. The computer self-test is necessary, but a complete equipment check-out goes further. A functional test, which involves running the equipment against a known standard, is good practice every time any machine is turned on.

If the functional test fails, adjust the machine and try again. If the machine runs successfully for two tests, the machine is probably okay. If either of the two tests fails, the machine should be declared suspect and either replaced or repaired immediately or double-checked continually while it is being used. This is rule-based sampling. The rule in this case is to validate the machine by testing the first one or two applications after each boot-up of the machine.

Random sampling may then be used for the rest of the run, but it clearly would not be likely to catch setup errors that would affect the first several applications until the first random sample was checked. Because of this, rule-based sampling has a role to play in any system.

Rule-based sampling is commonly applied if there is a known periodic behavior or conditioned behavior and only high (or low) values are of interest. Taking temperatures after an exercise period is likely to capture the highest temperature of the day. Taking the pulse rate at three o'clock in the morning is likely to get the lowest reading of the day. Rules based on the purpose of the measurement and the known periodic or conditioned behavior provide the key information with a minimum sampling effort.

Measurements of recovery time are commonly of interest. How long does it take for respiration rate to return to normal after five minutes of exercise? The recovery follows a known law, in this case an exponential curve, and samples taken during the recovery period can fix the parameters of the curve to sufficient precision. Other recovery processes may follow a different law (How long does it take the employee parking lot to clear out after the end of a shift?), but the law is usually pretty easy to discover by observation. If the law is known, a rule to guide any sampling can be developed in a straightforward way.

Work

1. Using the first data set below, set a rule for sampling that will give the highest readings during each cycle. Do this by picking a window of about five consecutive data points from the full data set when the readings are highest, then use the same window in the next cycle,

and so on. Next, pick a sampling plan that looks into this window, by rule, and takes a sufficient number of samples from that window to have a reasonable confidence that the average of the samples is not much less than the window average in the original data set. What confidence level seems reasonable to you? How are you going to apply the confidence level in this case, when only one side of the distribution is of interest?

2. Using the second data set below, which is an exponential recovery data set, pick a sampling plan that will give an average value, with reasonable confidence, for the first five minutes. From that average plus the reading at five minutes, the exponential parameter can be calculated. What confidence level seems to be reasonable?

Data

Use the following data sets; these can also be found on the companion web site, www.ache.org/pubs/barry/start.cfm.

Data set 1 includes data with a periodic component:

Data Set 1

21.0	20.6	21.0	21.2	20.4
21.3	21.8	21.4	21.8	21.8
21.8	22.2	21.9	22.6	22.3
23.4	22.9	23.0	22.9	22.7
23.7	23.1	23.8	23.5	23.3
23.6	24.1	24.3	23.8	24.1
24.9	24.0	24.4	24.1	24.3
24.8	24.8	24.6	24.3	24.8
25.1	24.5	24.8	24.6	25.4
24.8	24.7	24.9	24.9	24.9
24.7	24.8	25.4	25.0	24.7
24.3	24.9	25.0	25.1	24.6
24.5	24.6	24.5	24.2	24.3
24.3	23.7	24.2	23.9	23.6
23.0	23.3	23.3	23.2	23.7
22.9	23.0	22.9	22.9	22.6
22.0	22.8	22.6	22.4	22.0
21.3	21.2	21.3	21.8	21.5

(continued on following page)

(Continued)

Data Set 1				
20.3	21.1	20.7	20.6	21.0
19.7	20.0	20.4	19.9	20.1
19.1	19.0	18.8	19.0	18.7
18.3	18.3	18.6	18.4	18.4
17.8	17.7	17.4	18.2	18.1
17.2	17.1	16.9	16.7	16.9
16.2	16.0	16.8	16.8	16.9
16.2	15.9	16.1	15.5	15.8
15.7	15.3	16.0	15.8	15.1
15.2	15.4	14.9	15.3	15.4
15.5	14.9	15.3	14.9	14.8
15.3	15.4	15.4	14.6	15.2
15.2	15.4	15.0	14.7	15.1
15.6	15.5	15.6	15.6	15.7
15.6	15.6	15.6	15.1	15.1
16.0	16.4	16.1	15.7	16.2
16.4	16.0	16.3	16.6	16.6
17.5	17.5	16.6	17.5	17.0
18.1	17.3	17.5	17.8	17.5
18.3	18.4	18.7	18.6	18.3
19.3	19.0	18.7	19.7	19.5
20.2	19.9	19.5	19.5	20.2

Data set 2, exponential recovery, includes the times at which the values were read:

Data Set 2, Exponential Recovery (time given in seconds)					
Time	Value	Time	Value	Time	Value
6	41.0	54	40.6	102	40.3
12	40.9	60	40.6	108	40.3
18	40.9	66	40.6	114	40.3
24	40.8	72	40.5	120	40.2
30	40.8	78	40.5	126	40.2
36	40.7	84	40.4	132	40.2
42	40.7	90	40.4	138	40.1
48	40.7	96	40.4	144	40.1

(continued)

Time	Value	Time	Value	Time	Value
150	40.1	222	39.7	294	39.4
156	40.0	228	39.7	300	39.4
162	40.0	234	39.6	306	39.4
168	40.0	240	39.6	312	39.3
174	39.9	246	39.6	318	39.3
180	39.9	252	39.6	324	39.3
186	39.9	258	39.5	330	39.3
192	39.8	264	39.5	336	39.2
198	39.8	270	39.5	342	39.2
204	39.8	276	39.5	348	39.2
210	39.8	282	39.4	354	39.2
216	39.7	288	39.4	360	39.2

Analysis

In both of these cases, the time at which the samples are drawn may be important. Rule-based sampling plans that rely on extremely precise timing are obviously unworkable in the real world. For each of the above cases, estimate the effect, if any, if the readings are delayed by one time unit (one row). What if they are delayed by two time units? How many time units of delay do you estimate would be required to make a significant error in the result?

The work instructions for these cases have not specified any visualization charts. Reports generally have some charts, so pick out one or two that would portray the essence of each analysis.

Conclusion

The student will have developed sampling rules for periodic and exponential data sets. He or she will have considered the consequence of taking samples at delayed times, which has involved a departure from the original plan.

CASE 15: RICH DATA SETS

Topic: Classical Set Analysis

Much of this book has been devoted to dealing with limited data sets because in the real world, gathering data takes time and effort. However, occasions arise that bring an ocean of data, and the task for the analyst is to deal with the flood. If the data are already in computer files, the task is simplified to applying classical statistical analysis.

For example, if delivery times for x-rays to patient care units are recorded by time stamping and the time stamps flow into a computer file, there will be a flood of data.

Work

1. The data sets below record x-ray delivery times to different locations, labeled A, B, C, and D, in the building complex. Supervisors in location D assert that their service is materially worse than that provided to the other locations.

   Start with the null hypothesis that the service to D is the same as the service to A, then repeat with D and B, and again with D and C. Follow the next steps for each pair.

2. Select a high confidence level, say 90 percent, because management is involved.

3. Apply the TTEST(. . .) for each pair (D-A, D-B, and D-C) to see if the null hypothesis is valid for the average values. The TTEST function requires four arguments. The first two are the data sets to be compared; the remaining two set options for the analysis. Use values 2 and 3 for these options; these values mean, respectively, that both tails are to be considered and that the data sets have unequal standard deviations. So, if the data sets are in columns E and F, rows 12 through 97, the entry would be TTEST(E12:E97, F12:F97, 2, 3). This test returns a probability that the null hypothesis is true with regard to the average values of the data sets. Compare the result to the requirement of 90 percent confidence.

4. Apply the FTEST(. . .) to each pair to see if the null hypothesis is valid for the standard deviation. This test returns a probability that the null hypothesis is true with regard to the standard deviations of the data sets. Compare the result to the requirement of 90 percent confidence. The FTEST does not require any parameters, only the data sets.

5. Sort each data set, one at a time. Figure out where the top 10 percent cutoff is. (Hint: Count back 10 percent of the rows from the end of the set.) This cutoff represents the time to deliver 90 percent of the deliveries to each location. Compare these times. Repeat your

examination for the 75 percent and 50 percent cutoffs. Make a table of these so that they can be compared in a chart.

Data

Use this data set; it can also be found on the companion web site, www.ache.org/pubs/barry/start.cfm.

Item	A	B	C	D
1	22.8	16.3	19.4	22.2
2	22.4	19.3	20.6	22.6
3	18.7	20.3	21.6	22.2
4	14.9	25.2	18.6	21.3
5	21.7	20.7	18.5	23.1
6	18.2	15.4	20.7	21.8
7	17.7	19.3	21.8	23.0
8	20.8	19.6	20.6	21.4
9	22.7	14.9	22.6	21.8
10	19.7	20.7	22.2	22.0
11	17.0	26.4	19.6	22.9
12	19.4	17.6	23.0	21.6
13	20.0	22.7	23.6	22.2
14	19.4	24.8	17.6	21.9
15	18.8	16.4	18.6	22.0
16	21.1	19.4	16.5	22.0
17	16.6	16.5	18.1	21.2
18	18.0	16.6	19.9	21.7
19	15.8	21.9	18.4	21.5
20	17.0	20.3	17.6	21.7
21	14.4	21.8	21.8	21.5
22	16.2	22.8	21.8	22.3
23	19.1	18.3	21.8	21.2
24	17.6	19.8	21.4	21.5
25	28.8	15.4	20.9	22.5
26	19.2	16.9	20.3	22.3
27	19.0	17.4	19.5	22.5
28	21.4	23.9	20.4	21.4
29	16.1	15.6	20.4	21.4
30	19.4	22.5	20.2	20.8

(continued on following page)

Item	A	B	C	D
31	16.7	24.0	20.7	22.1
32	18.8	14.9	22.0	22.2
33	19.2	22.0	17.6	22.9
34	18.7	13.2	20.8	22.6
35	15.3	15.1	21.2	21.7
36	19.3	13.7	20.7	21.5
37	17.4	26.8	16.4	22.0
38	15.2	20.4	17.6	21.9
39	14.9	16.4	21.0	22.8
40	21.5	17.2	19.6	22.4
41	19.6	19.2	21.8	22.6
42	19.2	16.4	19.7	22.1
43	20.3	20.8	18.4	22.3
44	19.1	17.1	18.3	21.1
45	16.9	23.8	22.5	22.0
46	13.9	16.2	21.8	22.6
47	13.1	20.0	24.2	22.4
48	15.3	17.0	17.8	22.6
49	20.7	17.4	16.8	22.2
50	20.0	15.4	20.0	22.1
51	18.7	16.7	17.3	22.2
52	20.0	26.1	19.6	21.8
53	18.7	18.3	20.3	22.4
54	16.7	15.0	15.5	20.8
55	15.3	20.5	20.4	22.7
56	12.3	15.3	22.3	22.9
57	18.2	20.6	19.9	23.4
58	18.5	22.2	17.7	22.1
59	16.2	18.6	19.0	22.1
60	17.8	14.1	17.7	22.3
61	17.6	23.9	20.9	22.4
62	16.5	22.8	19.8	21.6
63	18.2	16.0	21.7	21.5
64	14.9	16.8	18.1	21.9
65	20.7	20.3	19.2	20.9
66	18.1	17.6	18.4	22.2
67	14.8	24.8	19.9	21.6

(continued)

Item	A	B	C	D
68	16.4	19.3	21.1	22.8
69	15.9	20.3	20.9	21.6
70	17.7	19.0	21.4	22.8
71	20.1	20.8	21.3	22.6
72	19.0	20.8	21.3	23.0
73	19.9	18.3	19.8	21.2
74	14.1	22.4	22.2	22.1
75	17.6	19.6	24.0	22.3
76	17.9	18.9	22.3	21.4
77	18.9	17.7	19.1	22.7
78	15.0	24.5	20.8	20.9
79	22.1	17.5	21.1	22.4
80	18.0	18.7	18.1	21.6
81	13.9	19.0	19.5	21.2
82	16.8	24.5	23.3	22.4
83	18.2	17.4	20.1	21.0
84	16.0	14.6	21.1	21.5
85	16.6	17.3	21.5	22.2
86	15.7	17.1	18.3	22.1
87	20.8	23.9	19.7	22.0
88	22.0	20.1	18.5	22.4
89	18.7	14.6	19.6	22.3
90	17.5	19.5	21.2	20.9
91	15.7	13.9	19.5	22.6
92	20.7	17.9	21.1	22.7
93	18.0	20.1	15.9	22.8
94	19.6	22.6	20.3	21.7
95	17.5	23.3	20.9	22.5
96	17.7	20.9	21.7	21.8
97	16.4	24.7	21.0	21.9
98	18.5	19.8	20.5	22.3
99	17.6	17.4	17.6	21.9
100	20.6	21.0	22.2	21.7

Analysis

What is the null hypothesis? In this case there are several null hypotheses, so state each one separately or else state the null hypothesis in a general way so as to include all possibilities. Is the null hypothesis supported to the confidence level required?

What location seems to be getting the best service on the basis of each of the measures? Is any significant difference found in the delivery times, and on what basis do you conclude that? Include a few charts in the report because this is a dispute among management, and therefore matters are not likely to be settled by pages of numbers.

Conclusion

The student will have applied classical statistical tests to rich data sets. He or she will also have selected suitable charts to portray the data and to support the conclusion.

CASE 16: SEQUENTIAL ANALYSIS

Topic: Acceptance Testing

Occasionally, you may have to decide that it is time to stop a test. Sequential testing supports an early decision on whether to accept a change. The method used here, while it may seem to be awfully simple, is just as rigorous as any other statistical method (Mood 1950).

The method to be applied here requires that the characteristics of the new distribution be known as well as the characteristics of the old distribution. The method can also be applied at the trial stage if the new distribution can be estimated. If new equipment is being evaluated to replace old equipment, the vendor of the new equipment may be able to supply the analyst with expected lifetime or failure rate. (Note: If the vendor provides inflated, optimistic lifetimes for the new equipment, this method will punish the new equipment in the evaluation.)

This method does not require that the new distribution and the old distribution be of the same form. If both are normal distributions, that is fine. If one is a normal distribution and the other a Weibull bathtub distribution, that is fine, too. If the distributions are not well known but enough data are available to make a histogram, that is good enough. Scale the histogram so that the sum of all probabilities is 100 percent.

Here is the method:

- Let the null hypothesis be that no difference exists between the old and the new distributions.
- Pick a confidence level against false negatives.
- Pick a confidence level against false positives.

(To review, a *false negative* is a rejection of the null hypothesis when the conclusion should have been to accept the null hypothesis. A *false positive* is an acceptance of the null hypothesis when the conclusion should have been to reject the null hypothesis. The *null hypothesis* is that no difference exists between the two distributions.)

Compute two limits:

- Limit A is the ratio of the false-positive confidence level to one minus the false-negative confidence level.
- Limit B is the ratio of one minus the false-positive confidence level to the false-negative confidence level.

For example, if the false-negative confidence level is 75 percent and the false-positive confidence level is 90 percent, Limit A is $90\%/(1 - 75\%)$, which equals 3.60, and Limit B is $(1 - 90\%)/75\%$, which equals 0.13. In general, Limit A will be greater than 1 and Limit B will be less than 1.

Gather the first sample. Evaluate the new distribution and the old distribution with this sample as the argument to the distribution function for each. Call these $V_{new,1}$ and $V_{old,1}$. Compute the ratio of $V_{new,1}$ to $V_{old,1}$, and call this $Ratio_1$.

Compare $Ratio_1$ to Limit A. If $Ratio_1$ is bigger than Limit A, *reject the null hypothesis.*

Compare $Ratio_1$ to Limit B. If $Ratio_1$ is smaller than Limit B, *accept the null hypothesis.*

If $Ratio_1$ is between the two, draw another sample. Do the same evaluations to get to a new ratio, which will be called $Ratio_2$. Multiply $Ratio_1$ by $Ratio_2$, and call this $Product_2$. Compare $Product_2$ to the limits, applying the same tests and drawing the same conclusions.

Repeat as many times as necessary, multiplying all the ratios together each time and doing the limit tests on that product. Hence, for example, $Product_4 = Ratio_4 \times Ratio_3 \times Ratio_2 \times Ratio_1$.

Compare $Product_4$ to Limit A. If $Product_4$ is bigger than Limit A, *reject the null hypothesis.*

Compare Product$_4$ to Limit B. If Product$_4$ is smaller than Limit B, *accept the null hypothesis.*

In theory, the first time either Limit A or Limit B is crossed, the evaluation sequence can be terminated and the conclusion announced. Because, in practice, the two distributions are never known with high precision, it is prudent to gather a few more samples to confirm the result.

Work

1. Apply this method to the evaluation of battery lifetime for a certain handheld computer device. A vendor has come forward with a new battery that he claims has a 30 percent greater life. This is the same vendor who sold you the old ones, and he offers you the parameters for the Weibull bathtub curve lifetime distribution, saying that his research laboratory has developed both the new and the old distributions based on extensive field and laboratory testing. Given that many users have complained about the short life of the old batteries and given that the price difference is small, you agree to conduct a trial test of the new batteries by putting them in 20 units and issuing them to regular users so that the tests will be representative.

2. The vendor asserts that the Weibull parameters for the old battery are 5 and 30, whereas the parameters for the new battery are 5 and 40. To see what this might look like, open a spreadsheet and evaluate the Weibull function for a range of values from 0 to 50. Work with the old battery data in one column and the new battery data in the next. Plot the results, showing both distributions on one chart, and include the chart in the report.

3. Start the trial. The first battery fails after 34 days. Apply the tests, using confidence limits of 80 percent and 90 percent for false-negative and false-positive tests. If the test is conclusive, declare victory. Applying the built-in Excel® function for the old distribution, WEIBULL(34,5,30,false), gives 4.24 percent, and for the new distribution, WEIBULL(34,5,40,false), gives 4.19 percent. Because the two are quite close together, one would expect the test to be inconclusive.

4. If the test is inconclusive, wait for the next battery to fail, and then apply the test to the product of the first two ratios as prescribed above.

5. Continue until one of the limits is crossed or until the trial population is exhausted.
6. Given that all of the 20 units are already in test, collect the battery life data as it comes in for all 20, and repeat the tests each time. Plot the products versus the failure-sequence number, and show the A and B limits on the plot. If the products get to be very large or very small, use some judgment about the plotting.

Data

Use this data set; it can also be found on the companion web site, www.ache.org/pubs/barry/start.cfm.

Sequence	Life	Sequence	Life
1	34.0	11	41.0
2	35.0	12	42.0
3	35.5	13	44.0
4	37.0	14	44.5
5	38.0	15	45.0
6	39.0	16	48.0
7	39.0	17	49.5
8	40.0	18	50.0
9	40.5	19	52.0
10	40.5	20	55.0

Analysis

The second parameter of the Weibull distribution is the lifetime parameter; 37 percent of all samples will have a lifetime greater than this parameter. For the new batteries, 37 percent can be expected to last to day 40. How does this compare with the actual results? For the old batteries, 37 percent can be expected to last to day 30. How does this compare with the actual results? On the basis of the actual lifetimes, would it be possible to choose between the two distributions? Suppose two of the batteries had been lost on day 35. Could this information be used in any way?

Conclusion

The student will have applied both false-negative and false-positive confidence tests to sequential data. He or she will have learned that use can be made of information about the new distribution if any is available.

CASE 17: RULE-INDUCED UPSETS

Topic: Management Effect on Service

This exercise will address local optimization versus global optimization. Management decides what is best for each patient while that patient is within the domain of that manager's unit and issues rules with the patient's best interest in mind. Each unit manager, however, has a focus of vision that is concentrated on that unit. Each manager cannot have the whole of the organization in mind at each moment. Therefore, each unit manager makes rules that look a lot like local optimizations, even with the best interest of the patient in mind.

In this case, the surgery unit does its routine surgery cases in the morning, and the patients are then held in the surgery unit, where they can get the best care in case of some difficulty, until 11:30 a.m. At this point, those patients showing standard progress are moved to the postoperative patient care unit for bedrest and further care.

On a typical day, 10 to 12 patients make this move. Three orderlies and three elevators are available, so the patients are delivered in groups of three. The orderlies get back to the surgery unit and return with the next set of three patients in five minutes.

Logging the patient in to the postoperative unit, getting the patient moved into the assigned room, and hooking up monitors and so on takes six minutes per patient. Two nurses are assigned to these tasks, and they work in parallel and draw on the patient care unit's aides and orderlies for help.

Work

1. Using a spreadsheet, tally the number of patients transferring into the postoperative pool at each minute. Tally the number moved out of the pool at each minute. Tally the pool count at each minute.

2. Calculate the average time, the 75 percent of population time, and the maximum time of patients' wait in the pool if 12 patients are being moved to postoperative care.
3. Analyze the data and create a chart or two to portray what is happening.

Data

No additional data are required for this case.

Analysis

Figuring that a long wait in the postoperative patient care unit pool to get to a bed is not the overall optimum situation for the patient, propose some different rules, equipment, or staffing that would likely improve this situation from the point of view of the patient. Draft a recommendation. Apply a simple potential problem analysis to the draft recommendation. Reconsider the recommendation in light of the potential problem analysis and, if appropriate, modify the recommendation somewhat. Include this recommendation in the report.

Does the recommendation affect more than one unit? If so, at what level in the organization does the recommendation have to reach?

Conclusion

The student will have considered unit operating rules that are in the best interest of the patient from the point of view of that unit. He or she will also have considered the effect on the next unit and will have recommended some change for consideration that addresses the best interest of the patient from a more global viewpoint.

CASE 18: IMPROVEMENT PROJECT

Topic: Snap-On Patient Monitors

A vendor proposes that the organization adopt the latest in snap-on patient monitors. This device fits over a thumb or a big toe and is connected by wire to a computer and then to the computer network; it monitors pulse rate, blood pressure, and gross changes in blood sugar level. The computer associates each device with an assigned patient, and it knows if the device has slipped off or has been moved in such a way as to lose its signals. The computer produces on-demand and on-trigger reports at the patient care unit station and can be accessed by authorized personnel using remote computer stations, two-way pagers, and other network devices.

The organization is already using some lower-functionality snap-on monitors on critical patients, but they are not being used for general patients because of the high cost of the older devices. The new devices are much cheaper and may be suitable for the general patient population.

The vendor has provided manufacturer's data supporting a claim that the failure rate of the new devices is very low (one-thousandth of the failure rate of the older devices), that the software failure rate is less than once in any five-year period, and that the patients in a test program in another state did not complain of discomfort while wearing the devices.

Work

1. Design a trial program for the new device. Consider what populations to include and consider where those populations are in the building complex. Do a potential problem analysis.
2. If the failure rate is truly low for the new device, and if the failure rate has been quite low for the older devices, on what basis will the trial be considered a success or failure? What quantitative analysis might you use? What data would you require for such quantitative analysis?
3. Make a recommendation to management.
4. Include your logic and some suitable charts in the report; maybe a process flow diagram would be useful, or maybe another type of diagram would be.

Data

No additional data are required for this case.

Analysis

One cost of the use of such devices on a regular basis is that small devices tend to get lost in the bedclothes and wander off in the pockets of discharged patients and visitors. Is this something to be considered in the design of the trial? If so, how would the trial take care of this?

If the trial is successful and the device is used very generally within the organization, what provisions should be made to deal with the exceptional patient who is allergic to the device or is bandaged in such a way that the device cannot be used?

Conclusion

The student will have considered a technology upgrade from one highly reliable generation of computerized equipment to the next. He or she will have designed a trial of the new generation principally on nonstatistical bases.

CASE 19: EVENT A

Topic: Bathroom Falls

A patient falls in the bathroom adjoining his room in the middle of the night. He suffers some minor injuries with no permanent consequences, but management, on consideration of the facts, decides that the same fall might have been life-threatening if the circumstances had been different in exceedingly minor ways. Management declares this to be a significant event and wants a solution. A project manager and analyst are assigned.

On reviewing the records for the past three years, it comes to light that 14 falls have occurred in patients' bathrooms, but none have resulted in serious injury. Some facts about each fall are given below.

Each patient's bed has rails, a call button, and a stepstool. Some patients are allowed to leave bed to go to the bathroom on their own, and some are not. These latter patients are said to be "restricted to bed." The difficulty with figuring out what to do to reduce errors in this case is that it is the patient who is making the error. Training the patient does not seem very promising as a solution.

This appears to be an opportunity to apply poka-yoke in an effort to develop a system that is so easy to use that even untrained people—in this case, patients—will be more likely to do the right thing than the wrong thing.

How can the bathroom-fall hazard be mitigated? Is there something about access to the bathroom that might be mitigating? Something inside the bathroom that might be mitigating? Something about getting out of bed, short of restraining every patient, that might be mitigating? Is there something about the patient being on his or her own that might be mitigating?

Work

1. Examine the data for patterns. Are any patterns evident?
2. Do a failure modes and effects analysis of the safety features already provided. Think poka-yoke.
3. Develop a trial program. Include a potential problem analysis. Include an analysis of the likely time duration of the trial.
4. Put the essentials in the report.

Data

Use the data given in the table below. Note that one fall may be counted in several different ways, so the totals exceed the number of individual falls.

Characteristic	Count of True	Count of False
Male	9	5
Elderly	10	4
First night in this bed and room	5	9
Restricted to bed	4	10
Used call button first	7	7
Had fallen before	1	13

Analysis

Does the proposed trial allow for a range of patient behaviors? Does the proposed trial rely on any change in patient behavior, and, if so, how will this be enforced? What sources of outside ideas should the analyst consider in seeking improvements for trial?

Conclusion

The student will have considered a matter where the error is not being made by the system but is being allowed by the system, with the actual error being made by a patient who cannot be controlled by the system short of bed restraints. He or she will have considered the poka-yoke approach to facilities design.

CASE 20: EVENT B

Topic: Pressure Ulcers

The organization provides bed care for periods of time typically running two to six weeks. Many patients have poor mobility. Some are subject to developing pressure ulcers (bed sores) if left by themselves in bed or in a wheelchair for extended periods of time. To reduce this likelihood, patients are turned in their beds twice each shift, and the patient may be awakened, if necessary, to do this. The patients are reseated in their wheelchairs during any extended chair time.

The turning is done by orderlies. This work is done mid-shift and again near the end of the shift. These orderlies have other duties assigned as well, some of which are highly variable in occurrence. The orderlies sign a sheet at the end of each round, marking each patient who has been turned or who, for some reason, has not been turned.

The organization finds that the number of pressure ulcer cases, although low, is not as low as the incidence rate reported by comparable organizations. Pressure ulcers are a serious matter on their own, and the incidence of pressure ulcers may detract from the organization's hard-won reputation for giving good care. Management decides to take this matter seriously, even though this issue is not thought to be life-threatening. A project manager and analyst are assigned.

On review of the records, the project team decides that the existing policy is the right one and that something is going wrong in its implementation. What is needed is not a new policy but the same policy, and yet clearly a problem exists. What needs to be done?

Work

1. Do a failure modes and effects analysis.
2. Recommend a new trial of the present process.
3. Recommend appropriate trial measures.
4. Include a chart or two in the report.

Data

No additional data are required for this case.

Analysis

What long-term tracking do you recommend?

Conclusion

The student will have applied the Six Sigma method to the rectification—rather than the improvement—of a process.

WORKFLOW CASES

These cases are not part of the standard Six Sigma green belt and black belt training programs. They are included here for the amusement and enlightenment of our readers.

The Amusement Park Workflow Case Set

1. You are the manager of an amusement park. You have recently switched to all-you-can-ride admission pricing. Now you find that half your customers want to ride your Really Big Roller Coaster and have to stand in line for an hour to get on the ride. While they are waiting, they are thinking vile things about you and, what is worse, they are not buying anything at the concession stands.

   Think up three things that you could do to alleviate the problem. Make arguments for each.

   Is this bunching, batching, pending, or queuing?

2. You find that at least one-quarter of those who ride the Really Big Roller Coaster get right back in line to ride it again. You would like to accommodate them because they are probably your best customers and are most likely to come to the park again soon, but you would like to make sure everyone who wants to ride the coaster gets at least one chance to do so.

   Think up three things you could do to ensure fair treatment for each customer who wants to ride the coaster.

3. Draw a time-value diagram from the point of view of the customer who is a coaster fan. Consider the admission fee payment a negative value. Use your imagination for values to ascribe to riding the coaster, riding the carousel, and so on. Consider the purchase of a hotdog as a small positive value.

4. Draw a time-value diagram from the point of view of the owner of the amusement park. The admission fee has value to you. What else has value to you while the customer is in the park? Is keeping the customer in the park a positive or a negative to you?

5. Your customers drive to your amusement park and park in your lot. On busy days, parking takes a while because of the crush of incoming cars in addition to the manner in which you want people to park. Because of this, several bottlenecks are possible in customer flow: getting parked, getting admitted, getting on the roller coaster, and getting out of the parking lot to go home.

   Because everything is under your control, you can force one of these to be the true bottleneck. Consider where you want the bottleneck to be. Defend your selection.

   How would you know whether your bottleneck management scheme is working?

6. To improve capacity, you consider breaking the four-car roller coaster train down into two two-car trains. You know that the ride time will still be five minutes. The reloading time will be two minutes because this time is dictated by the slowest-moving passenger.

   Will making this change improve capacity? (Hint: Draw a time-value sketch for the four-car train, then draw additional traces for the two two-car trains. What fraction of the time is each car in action?)

7. You have two more cars in storage. If you bring them out and put them in service, should it be as extra cars on one long train, as a separate two-car train, or as third cars on the existing two-car trains? Loading time will still be two minutes per train, regardless of train length. (Hint: Make more time-value sketches. Try a time-value sketch for the track.)

8. Your brother-in-law wants to open a soft drink concession stand just at the exit walkway from the Really Big Roller Coaster because he thinks this will catch a lot of customers who are excited from the ride. If he is right, about half of the coaster riders will stop at

the new stand. Given that the passengers all come away from the coaster in a bunch, how many customers does the new stand have to serve, and how many minutes do they have to get the service done? Does it matter if the coaster is running one long train or two or three smaller trains? Is this bunching, batching, pending, or queuing?

9. Sodas jerks at the new stand can serve one customer every 30 seconds. People will not stand in line if the line already has more than three people in it. How many soda jerks should the stand have? Why?

10. The stand can either have the soda jerks handle payment, or it can have a separate cashier. If the soda jerks only have to jerk sodas, they can serve a customer every 20 seconds. The cashier can handle eight people per minute. Is one cashier enough? (Hint: Draw a time-value curve from the point of view of the customer. Considering queuing time to get the soft drink, work time to get the soft drink, queuing time to get to the cashier, and work time to pay the cashier.)

11. Cashiers are paid more than soda jerks. Customer service is more important than labor cost. Does that figure into the staffing strategy?

Appendices

These appendices provide additional information. It has been gathered here to facilitate the flow of information in the regular text. Selected formulae, an annotated bibliography, and a glossary are provided.

SELECTED FORMULAE

These formulae have been selected for inclusion here because they underlie the statistical analysis provided these days by computer applications. These are included for information only; familiarity with them is not required to follow the text nor to apply the Six Sigma method.

The cumulative uniform distribution

$$F(x; a, b) = \int_a^x \frac{dx}{b - a}$$

The cumulative normal distribution

$$F(x; \mu, \sigma) = \int_{-\infty}^x \frac{1}{\sqrt{2\pi}\sigma} e^{-(x-\mu)^2/2\sigma^2} dx$$

The cumulative gamma distribution

$$F(x; \alpha, \beta) = \int_0^x \frac{1}{\alpha! \beta^{\alpha+1}} t^\alpha e^{-t/\beta} dt$$

The cumulative Poisson distribution

$$F(x'; \lambda) = \sum_0^{x'} \frac{e^{-\lambda} \lambda^x}{x!}$$

The cumulative Student's t distribution

$$F(t;n) = \int_{-\infty}^{t} \frac{\left(\dfrac{n-1}{2}\right)!}{\left(\dfrac{n-2}{2}\right)!\sqrt{\pi n}\left(1+\dfrac{x^2}{n}\right)^{(n+1)/2}} \, dx$$

EFFECT OF PRECISION IN LOW-COUNT ESTIMATING

Estimating the standard distribution of a set of samples is necessary to apply the process control limits and system limits discussed in the text. When the sample count is high (more than 20), the classical formula executed by the Excel® function STDEV(. . .) gives a result that is sufficiently precise for practical use.

When the sample count is low, caution is in order. The Excel® formula will return an answer with a sample count as low as two. Just having a result, though, is not the whole story. It is necessary to have an understanding of whether that result is sufficiently precise as to justify its use.

The diagram below shows the 50 percent confidence intervals for the standard deviation of a set of samples. The samples are random numbers generated from a normal distribution that has mean value of zero and standard deviation of unity. So, in this case, we know that the standard deviation estimations should be close to unity if the estimation process is any good. The estimating was repeated 100 times, and an average value was computed using the chi-square distribution for the upper and lower limits on the confidence interval. This was done for sample counts of 2, 5, 10, and 20.

The confidence interval does not represent a single-number estimate of the target (in this case the standard deviation of the underlying population) but rather a range of values that *probably* includes the target value. In this case, the confidence level is only 50 percent, so a prudent gambler would only bet even money that this range includes the target value. This is a pretty weak screen.

Even so, the figure clearly shows that the confidence interval is quite wide when the sample count is low. As the sample count increases, the confidence interval shrinks; this always happens. If the sample count were increased again, the confidence interval would shrink again.

If a *higher* confidence level were stipulated, the confidence intervals would be *larger* in all cases.

Another estimation method is cited by authors of engineering texts (Montgomery 1991; Breyfogle 1999) and is included here for completeness but without any recommendation that it be used in practice. This method is easy to do by hand, but then little is done by hand these days. This method proceeds as follows:

Take a sample set. Find the maximum value and the minimum value, and take the difference between the two. Call this the *range*. Multiply the range by the number from the following table. Use the result as an estimate of the standard deviation of the distribution.

Sample Count	Multiplier
2	0.8865
5	0.4299
10	0.3249
15	0.2880
20	0.2677
25	0.2544

The result of this range method is included in the graph below. It will be seen that the range method gives a better estimate when the count is two, but otherwise the range method and the classical method give about the same result. When the sample count is only two, both methods give a poor estimate, so the better course of action is to get more data.

FIGURE A1: CLASSICAL AND RANGE-BASED CONFIDENCE INTERVALS ON THE STANDARD DEVIATION

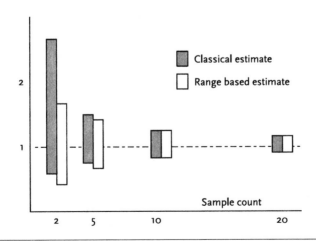

A poor estimate is sometimes better than no estimate at all. When in need of an estimate with only a small number of samples to work from, the prudent analyst makes the estimate using the data available and improves the estimate as more data come to hand, being cautious in the meantime.

EFFECT OF IGNORING MULTIPLE ERRORS IN ESTIMATING YIELD

The overall system first-time-through yield is the product of the first-time-through yields of the stages of service. Counting errors is easier than counting successes if the error rate is low, and the error rate is related to the yield. To a good approximation, that is, by ignoring those cases in which multiple errors occurred, the yield and the error rate add to 100 percent.

It may be useful to consider the effect of several errors showing up in the same patient's file. Surely, if it is possible to have one error, it must be possible to have two or three or more errors, considering that there are hundreds of opportunities for error in a patient's file, no matter how low the error rate is.

Case 5 poses the situation that the accounting error rate is 25 per million, with 200 accounting entries in the file. In addition, there is a treatment error rate of seven per million, with 500 opportunities for treatment error per patient.

Consider the accounting error prospects. Numerically, this is the same as having a very large bag with one million marbles in it of which 25 are red and the rest blue. We go to this bag 200 times, pulling one marble each time, noting its color, and putting the drawn marble back in the bag with a good shake so that we do not pull the same marble again the next draw. After 200 draws, what will our tally show? It might show all red, it might show all blue. It might show something in between.

There is a mathematical formula for determining the outcomes, and it is called the binomial distribution. Excel® provides a built-in function to calculate the likelihood that any selected number of marbles will be blue. For example, what is the likelihood that the tally will show that exactly three of the marbles drawn were red?

For calculating first-time-through yield, our interest is in the likelihood that the number of red marbles (representing error) is zero. So, we call on the Excel® function and evaluate:

BINOMDIST(0, 200, 25E-6, false) = 99.5012%.

The first argument is our tally of interest, namely zero events; the second argument is the number of tries, in this case 200. The third argument is the error rate, with the "E-6" being a shorthand way of entering "per million"; this could also have been entered as 0.000025. The fourth argument says to return just the likelihood for this specific tally of interest, not all the tallies to the left. Because this tally is zero, there are no tallies to the left anyway, so it does not matter what is entered here.

Calculating probabilities to six digits is usually excessive because the parameters are only known to a couple of digits. In this case, all those digits are of some interest because we wish to compare this "exact" calculation to the simple approximation used in Case 5; we are trying to see if the yield is one minus the expected error rate.

The number of errors expected is the error rate times the number of opportunities for error, or 25 per million multiplied by 200, which equals 5,000 per million, or 0.5 percent.

We will try the simple approximation: if the number of errors expected is 0.5 percent, the first-time-through yield is 100 percent minus 0.5 percent, which equals 99.5 percent.

Comparing this simple approximation to the exact calculation is to compare 99.5 percent to 99.5012 percent. Surely this is a negligible difference.

Applying the same method to the treatment error expectations from Case 5, with an error rate of seven per million and 500 opportunities for error, gives the following:

The exact calculation [BINOMDIST(0, 500, 7E-6, false)] results in 99.6506 percent, and the simple approximate value (100% − 7 per million × 500) results in 99.65 percent. Again, the difference is trivial.

For the combined two-step process, the yield is calculated as the product of the per-stage yields, which is 99.5012 percent × 99.6506 percent, or 99.1536 percent. The simple approximation takes the product of the two approximate per-stage yields, which is 99.5 percent × 99.65 percent, or 99.1518 percent. If the errors per stage are simply added, they are 500 per million and 350 per million for a total of 850 per million. Subtracting 850 per million from 100 percent gives 99.15 percent. The differences between the two approximations and the exact value are surely negligible.

The same can be said about applying these approximations to more stages of a process. As long as the error rate is low, the approximations are good enough for almost any purpose. If the error rate is high (more than 10 percent), using the built-in functions of a spreadsheet works best to reduce this contribution to uncertainty.

Even when using the exact formula, it is best to round the answer off to the same number of digits as the least-well-known parameter used as an argument to the function. If the inputs are only known to about three places, the answer is only reliable to about three places, no matter how many places the computer puts into the spreadsheet cell. This can be shown by experimenting with small differences in the input parameters to the function.

EFFECT OF IGNORING NEGATIVE VALUES IN DISTRIBUTIONS

The normal distribution accepts arguments that run to negative infinity, so the application of the normal distribution to populations that cannot possibly have negative values involves some error. If the bulk of the population is far to the right of zero, the error is obviously negligible. If the bulk of the population is not too far to the right of zero, maybe the error is not negligible after all.

It is so convenient to use the normal distribution—and so inconvenient to calculate adjustment factors—that it is worth some small effort to determine if the errors are appreciable in practical cases. The conclusion will be that the error is small and that no appreciable effect results from applying the normal distribution for Six Sigma applications.

ADJUSTING THE NORMAL DISTRIBUTION FOR POSITIVE-ONLY POPULATIONS

For a continuous distribution such as the normal distribution, the area under the distribution curve must, by definition, be unity. To the extent that part of the area is excluded, the remaining distribution needs to be adjusted upward to get back to a total area of unity.

The size of this adjustment depends on the size of the excluded area. If the excluded area is small, the adjustment is small. The size of the excluded area depends on the offset between the origin and the average point of the normal distribution, which is conveniently measured in standard deviation units. The following table gives the adjustment factor tabulated against that offset:

Adjustment Factor to Account for Exclusion of the Negative Half-Plane

Offset in Standard Deviation Units	Adjustment Factor
1	1.189
2	1.023
3	1.001
4	1.000
5	1.000
6	1.000

It is clear that the adjustment factor is significant if the offset is on the order of one standard deviation, but it falls off rapidly as the offset grows.

This adjustment factor applies to the elevation of the normal curve and acts to make the curve "higher" in the right half-plane to account for the exclusion of the left half-plane. With the adjustment factor applied, the area under the normal curve is unity.

The altitude of the distribution curve is of some interest, but the interest is greater in the region of the upper system limit, which is at least 4.5 standard deviations to the right of the average point. It is required that the tail of the distribution falling to the right of the upper system limit be not greater than 3.4 per million.

The effect on the tail of the adjusted distribution, to the right of 4.5 standard deviations, is tabulated against the size of the offset in the following table:

Tail of the Adjusted Normal Distribution to the Right of the Upper System Limit

Offset from the Origin	Tail in Parts per Million
1	4.04
2	3.48
3	3.41
4	3.40
5	3.40
6	3.40

If the adjustment factor is ignored and the normal curve is used without adjustment, the error is greatest for low offset, and it is less than one part per million as compared with the 3.4 parts per million objective when the offset is one standard deviation unit. For two or more standard deviations of offset, the error is even smaller.

Therefore, for Six Sigma purposes, ignore the adjustment results in only a negligible error of less than one part per million.

USING THE NORMAL DISTRIBUTION IN PLACE OF THE POISSON DISTRIBUTION

The Poisson distribution is a discrete distribution. It has only one parameter, which is the average value, and this value is also the square of the standard deviation for the distribution. When that parameter is large, the Poisson distribution takes on the familiar bell-shaped curve and is hardly distinguishable from a normal curve with the same average and standard deviation.

When the Poisson parameter is small, the shape is less like a bell curve and is more tilted to the right. Using a normal curve to approximate this asymmetric shape may introduce error.

The Poisson curve, because it is discrete, takes on only values equal to the natural numbers plus zero. No negative values are possible. To compare a normal distribution, which is continuous, with a Poisson distribution, which is discrete, some arrangement must be made to harmonize the two. In the following chart, to make the normal distribution into an equivalent discrete distribution, all points between 1.5 and 2.5 will be associated with the discrete value 2, all points between 2.5 and 3.5 will be associated with the discrete value 3, and so on. For zero, the associated area is between +0.5 and −0.5.

Because the negative half-plane is excluded to the left of the −0.5 point, there may be a question of the size of any error introduced if any such adjustment is ignored. There are two matters of interest: how well the probabilities compare, and how well the tails at 4.5 standard deviations compare.

The comparative distributions can be seen in the following chart, in which the Poisson and normal curves have the average value of one. The x-axis counts from zero and goes to the right in units of the standard deviation, which is itself unity.

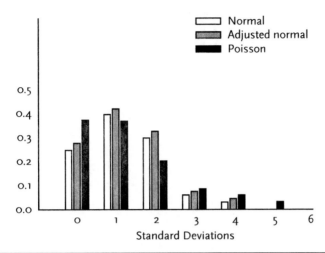

It will be seen that the Poisson distribution is noticeably higher than the normal curves at the zero point and somewhat lower than the normal curves thereafter. If the zero point is of particular interest (as it may be in low error rate comparisons), using a normal approximation to the Poisson may be a poor choice.

To consider the Six Sigma interest of the size of the tail to the right of the upper system limit (which is at least 4.5 standard deviations to the right of the average value), consider the following table, which has average values and standard deviation values of unity for both distributions:

Tail Beyond Upper System Limit

Unadjusted Normal Distribution	Poisson Distribution
3.4 per million	594 per million

These tail sizes are rather different and may not permit the normal approximation to the Poisson distribution when the average value is one.

To see if the disagreement persists when the average values are larger than one, and taking into account that the standard deviation will be the square root of the average value to conform to the Poisson definition, here is another table:

Tail Beyond Upper System Limit

Offset	Unadjusted Normal, Parts per Million	Poisson, Parts per Million
1	3.4	594
2	3.4	237
5	3.4	69
10	3.4	47
20	3.4	25
50	3.4	21

This table shows that, although the discrepancy falls for larger offsets, it does not disappear even for an offset of 50. Whether this discrepancy is significant in any analysis depends on the circumstances and cannot be assessed in general terms.

Conclusions

The error made in using a normal distribution as an approximation to the Poisson distribution exceeds 500 parts per million in Six Sigma analysis, for an average value of one. The discrepancy falls with rising average value, but the discrepancy is still more than 20 parts per million, for an average value of 20. The error is such that the normal approximation is optimistic and not conservative in this regard.

Even so, the normal approximation is often used where more careful analysis would apply the Poisson distribution, on the assumption that the central limit theorem will take care of any difficulties.

Annotated Bibliography

The literature on quality improvement in healthcare is extensive, and the literature on applied statistical methods is nearly as extensive. The following are sources used in this book, but this is not a complete nor even a partial listing of all sources that may be of interest. The comments are offered with the intent to be helpful to the reader and are not meant as estimations of the works themselves. Indeed, these works are highly esteemed, or else they would not appear here.

Aguayo, R. 1990. *Dr. Deming, the American Who Taught the Japanese about Quality*. Secaucus, NJ: Lyle Stuart.

> Case studies offered by a consultant who worked with Deming. Despite the title, the book is not a biography.

American Nurses Association. 2000. *Nursing Quality Indicators Beyond Acute Care* and *Measurement Instruments and Nursing Quality Indicators Beyond Acute Care*. Literature review. Washington, DC: American Nurses Association.

> These two reports issue from the American Nurses Association and support recommendations made by the ANA with regard to means to improve the quality of healthcare. The particular point is that overemphasis on cost reduction impinges on the quality of healthcare if nursing and other standards are not honored.

Breyfogle, F. W. III. 1999. *Implementing Six Sigma, Smarter Solutions Using Statistical Methods*. New York: Wiley.

> This is a thorough presentation of Six Sigma for factory applications for an engineering audience and includes equations, tables, and drills. The text brings Henry James to mind.

Breyfogle, F. W. III, Cupello, J. M., and Meadows, B. 2001. *Managing Six Sigma, A Practical Guide to Assessing, and Implementing, the Strategy that Yields Bottom-Line Success*. New York: Wiley.

This book is intended for managers and is nearly equation-free. It describes why and how to apply Six Sigma and includes a few case studies. It is a well-written text with the intent to cover service industries as well as manufacturing industries, but the service industries are limited to transaction processors.

Chicago Historical Society and the Trustees of Northwestern University. 1996. "The Great Conflagration." www.chicagohs.org/fire/conflag/.

Narration of the Chicago fire by witnesses plus extracts from the *Chicago Tribune*, whose brand-new fireproof office tower in the center of the city burned to the ground. The records show that the fire started in or near the O'Leary barn. The cow is folklore, but somebody must have kicked over the lantern, wouldn't you agree?

Crosby, P. 1979. *Quality is Free.* New York: McGraw-Hill.

This book reawakened American industry to quality as a business interest. It's free! Many found it to be so. Six Sigma derives directly from Crosby's work, which focuses on getting rid of errors, albeit with less specificity than Six Sigma applies. Crosby declared that quality is the satisfaction of requirements and nothing else, and this is an important point in the development of Six Sigma.

Emerson, R. W. 1860. "Culture." In *The Conduct of Life,* ch. IV. Revised 1876.

A fuller citation is more amusing, not something one seeks in Emerson as a rule: "Colonel, that none but a poltroon will boast that he never was afraid. A great part of courage is the courage of having done the thing before."

Gaba, D. M., Fish, K. J., and Howard, S. K. 1994. *Crisis Management in Anesthesiology.* Philadelphia: Harcourt.

Dr. Gaba is a pioneer in reducing error in anesthesiology, and in this book he catalogs special events and how to handle them.

Gilbreth, F., Jr., and Gilbreth, E. 1950. *Cheaper by the Dozen.* Reissued 1984. Chicago: Dramatic Publishing Company.

Delightful story of the authors' parents, Frank and Lillian Gilbreth, efficiency experts, and their 12 children before World War I. Not much about their professional work, but then if you've seen one stopwatch, you've seen them all. The movie (MGM 1950) has online reviews at www.rinkworks.com/movies/m/cheaper.by.the.dozen.1950.shtml.

The Gilbreth professional work is cited at www.accel-team.com/
scientific/scientific_03.html.

Goldratt, E. M., and Cox, J. 1984. *The Goal*. New York: North River Press,
Croton-on-Hudson.

Everyone should write like this! It's a novel; the hero discovers Goldratt's principles as he struggles with factory problems familiar to
any industrialist. There are no equations. Goldratt is a mathematician
who elaborated the mathematical principles underlying the Japanese
Kanban/low inventory system, which is the foundation of workflow
analysis used in this book. Highly recommended for all audiences
and all managers, particularly in healthcare.

Gribbin, H. 2002. "Hospital Health Hazard." *The Washington Times*,
February 10.

Gribbin cites Occupation Safety and Health Administration and other
federal reports on the incidence of assaults in emergency rooms, psy-
chiatric hospitals, and elsewhere. In the 1980s, at least 106 healthcare
workers died as the result of assault.

Hansen, D. A. 2001. *Total Quality Management (TQM) Tutorial/Help
Page*. http://home.att.net/~iso9k1/tqm/tqm.html.

A useful general source of information on total quality management,
including 10-step and 14-point lists, six types of charts, and other
quick information.

Joint Commission on Accreditation of Healthcare Organizations. 1998.
Sentinel Events: Evaluating Cause and Planning Improvement, 2nd ed.
Chicago: Joint Commission.

This is an analysis of life-threatening events and a workbook for
dealing with such incidents.

———. 2001. *2001 Hospital Accreditation Standards*. Oakbrook Terrace,
IL: Joint Commission.

Joint Commission standards are voluntary; they are issued for hospitals and a variety of other healthcare organizations.

Juran, J. M. 1995. *Managerial Breakthrough*, revised ed. New York:
McGraw-Hill.

One of the very best books for management on both the why and the
how of quality as a competitive weapon. Juran is one of the founders
of the modern quality movement and should be read for that reason

alone. It is also a good book that gets right to the point, and it has been written for managers, not statisticians.

Kazandjian, V. A. (ed.). 1997. *The Effectiveness of CQI in Health Care.* Milwaukee: ASQC Quality Press.

A compendium of reports on healthcare quality projects from the expected places (Holland, Japan, and others) and from some surprising ones, such as Niger.

Kirk, R. 1997. *Managing Outcomes, Process, and Cost in a Managed Care Environment.* Gaithersburg, MD: Aspen.

A how-to book on applying quality programs in the healthcare arena with forms, charts, and step-by-step instructions. Witty and easy to follow, this book is closer to total quality management than to other regimens.

Leveson, N. G. 1995. *Safeware, System Safety and Computers.* New York: Addison Wesley.

This book deals with ultra-reliable software system design for NASA and reports on safety event analysis in aviation and other industries.

Mango, P. D., and Shapiro, L. A. 2001. "Hospitals Get Serious About Operations." *The McKinsey Quarterly* 2: 74–85.

McKee, M. K. 2002. "Intensive Care." With S. Swanson. *Information Week* June 17, p. 20.

The article features Xerox as a company focusing on computerization of physicians' orders as a way to serve mankind and shareholders at the same time.

McLaughlin, C. P., and Kalunzny, A. D. 1994. *Continuous Quality Improvement in Health Care.* Gaithersburg, MD: Aspen.

An introduction to quality principles from Deming, Crosby, Juran, and others. Case studies in healthcare are contributed by various authors. The test at the end of the book blends total quality management and continuous quality improvement.

Meisenheimer, C. G. 1997. *Improving Quality, a Guide to Effective Programs,* 2nd ed. Gaithersburg, MD: Aspen.

Excellent history of quality initiatives in healthcare since 1900. It includes the standards of the Joint Commission and compares quality assurance with quality improvement.

Miller, R., Desmarais, J., and Calvaruso, J. T. 2001. "Six Sigma—The Quest for Quality." *Hospitals & Health Networks*. www.hhnmag.com.

Montgomery, D. C. 1991. *Introduction to Statistical Quality Control*, 2nd ed. New York: Wiley.
> This is the standard engineering textbook on applied statistics. It is a technique and applications text, not a guide to quality management, but it is an excellent technical reference book.

Mood, A. M. 1950. *Introduction to the Theory of Statistics*. New York: McGraw-Hill.
> This graduate-level statistics text was written before computers were common, back when it was necessary to think things through.

Murphy, Edward A. Air Force Captain. 1949.
> Namesake of Murphy's Law.

National Institute of Standards and Technology. 2001. *Malcolm Baldrige Criteria for Health Care 2001*. Washington, DC: National Institute of Standards and Technology.
> Formerly known as the Bureau of Standards, the National Institute for Standards and Technology also issues criteria for the Baldrige Awards in other industries. Visit the Institute's website at www.nist.gov/.

Parkinson, C. N. 1957. *Parkinson's Law*. Boston: Houghton Mifflin.
> Hilarious research into bureaucratic wonts.

Peter, L. J. 1979. *Peter's People and Their Marvelous Ideas*. New York: William Morrow.
> This book includes not only the Peter Principle but scores of other "laws" and aphorisms that are delightful as well as instructive. See also *The Peter Pyramid*, published in 1986.

Peters, T. J., and Waterman, R. H., Jr. 1982. *In Search of Excellence*. New York: Harper & Row.
> This book is the timely story of a collection of companies that were trying hard to do things right. It is the first of a series of such books by Peters. Peters makes the point that the Excellent Companies, by their very striving, ignite a passion in their employees.

Rosander, A. C. 1991. *Deming's 14 Points Applied to Services*. New York: Marcel Dekker.
> Case studies of Deming applications, but not in healthcare.

Ryan, M. J. R., and Thompson, W. P. 1998. *CQI and the Renovation of an American Health Care System*. Milwaukee: Quality Press.

    The story of one large health system's progress through applied continuous quality improvement; it also deals with intangibles and the challenges of managing a multisite group.

Shingo, S. 1981. *Study of the Toyota Manufacturing System*. Tokyo: Japanese Management Association.

    Case studies in rapid setup, small batch, Kanban manufacturing, and the progressive substitution of machine effort for human effort; poka-yoke is the recurring error-reduction method.

Statsoft. http://www.statsoft.com/textbook/stathome.html.

    Statsoft, a commercial provider of statistical software, provides a very good introductory-level online software textbook.

Student (Gosset, W. S.). 1908. "The Probable Error of a Mean." *Biometrica* 6: 1–25.

Taguchi, G. 1978. "Off-line and On-line Quality Control Systems." In *Proceedings of the International Conference on Quality Control*, pp. B4-1–B4-5. Tokyo: International Conference on Quality Control.

    Taguchi introduced the important idea of uniform satisfaction of requirements, which is key to Six Sigma.

Taylor, F. W. 1911. *The Principles of Scientific Management*. New York: Harper.

    This is the original efficiency-by-stopwatch book, but most of Taylor's gains in productivity were through improved ergonomics.

Walton, M. 1986. *The Deming Management Method*. Boston: Perigee Books.

    Walton worked with Deming and provides a readable book with many Deming anecdotes.

———. 1990. *Deming Management at Work*. Boston: Perigee Books.

    Case studies of the Deming method, including a case study of the Hospital Corporation of America and others from Ford Motor Company to the U.S. Navy. Perhaps the most interesting case is Tri-Cities, Tennessee, where a whole region tried to apply Deming's principles to every company in the region.

Glossary

Topic	Discussion
A priori, a posteriori	Before the fact, after the fact; sometimes written with hyphens or italicized for clarity
ANOVA	Analysis of variance
Average	The arithmetic sum of the values in a set divided by the number of members of the set
Baldrige Award	Federal quality award named for the Honorable Malcolm Baldrige, formerly U.S. Secretary of Commerce
Bathtub curve	A distribution that is high at both ends and low in the middle, faintly reminiscent of the shape of a bathtub
Chi-square distribution	The distribution of a variate defined as the square of the ratio of (the difference between a sample value and the sample average value) to the standard deviation of the underlying distribution
Clinical pathways	A systematic method for studying workflow in a healthcare organization
Confidence interval	An interval in which, to a specified level of confidence, a parameter being estimated lies
Confidence level	An a priori probability to be associated with a confidence interval

(continued on following page)

Topic	Discussion
Control chart	A chart that portrays sample values plotted against sample number or time
Degrees of freedom	The number of samples available
Expectation	The probability of a specified outcome
F distribution	The distribution of a variate that is the ratio of two variables independently distributed by chi-square distributions
False negative	The finding of a negative outcome in a trial that is false; finding false when the outcome should have been true
False positive	The finding of a positive outcome in a trial that is false; finding true when the outcome should have been false
Histogram	A chart showing the frequency of occurrence of each of several outcomes
ISO, ISO 9000	International Standards Organization standards in the 9000 group, which have to do with quality assurance; the International Standards Organization issues standards on many topics
Joint Commission on Accreditation of Healthcare Organizations	Joint Commission on Accreditation of Healthcare Organizations, Oakbrook Terrace, Illinois, 60181.
Kanban	Production on demand, particularly in small-batch production; the name is the Anglicized form of the Japanese word for "punched card"
Keisen, Kaizen	Anglicized version of the Japanese term for "continuous improvement." Many English spellings are used.

(continued)

Topic	Discussion
Law, in statistics	A rule governing behavior of a variate
Likelihood	Probability of a specific outcome
Mean	See *average*
Murphy's Law	Anything that can go wrong will go wrong
Normal distribution	The commonly occurring bell-shaped distribution, the equation for which uses the negative exponential of a squared variate; elaborated on by Gauss
Pareto Principle	An 80/20 rule of thumb; for example, 80 percent of sales come from 20 percent of the customer base
Parkinson's Law	Work expands to fill the time available; there are many variations on this law
Peter Principle	Managers are promoted to their level of incompetence, which is defined as one level beyond their level of competence
poka-yoke	The systematic design of work tasks so that the worker finds it easier to do the right thing than the wrong thing, rendering any error immediately obvious, and providing opportunity for errors to be rectified on the spot; "mistake-proofing"
Population	The count of, or the definition of, a discrete group; for example, the population of patients, x-ray files, or magnetic resonance imaging machines

(continued on following page)

Topic	Discussion
Probability	The ratio of the number of occurrences of a specific outcome to the number of all possible outcomes; a probability is always between zero and one. For example: the probability of drawing the jack of clubs from a pack is 1 in 52; the probability of drawing a jack of any suit is 4 in 52; the probability of drawing a club of any rank is 13 in 52; the probability of the drawn card being a jack, given that it is a club, is 1 in 13; the probability of the drawn card being a club, given that it is a jack, is 1 in 4; the probability of drawing the same card twice in a row is 1 in 52
Process control limits	Lines drawn for convenience on a control chart, displaced three standard deviations from the average value. These are convenient because data points will fall outside these lines only about once in 1,000 times if the process is following a normal distribution with fixed parameters; any point outside the control limits is unlikely and therefore suspect
Quality assurance	The administration of the production process with a view toward producing consistent outcomes
Regression	Fitting a selected equation to data samples; for example, linear regression fits a straight line
Residual	The square of the difference in values between a sample and its expected value calculated from some equation, usually an equation fitted to the data samples

(continued)

Topic	Discussion
Rich data set	A data set with a large number of data points, usually at least 50
Scientific management	The study of work, tasks, human behavior in the workplace, the flow of work, and related matters with emphasis on quantification
Sigma	Greek letter that is commonly used, in lower case, to represent the standard deviation
Significance	A measure of an unlikely outcome; an outcome that is significant at the 0.05 level would be expected to happen only 5 percent of the time; the significance level and the confidence level together add up to 100 percent
Six Sigma	A management method to reduce errors to the specific level of 3.4 errors per million in practical organizations
Sparse data set	A data set with only a few data points, usually less than 25
Standard deviation	The square root of the variance
Student's t distribution	The distribution of a variate that is the ratio of a normally distributed variate to the square root of a variate independently distributed by the chi-square law; this is valuable because a priori knowledge of the standard deviation of the underlying distribution is not needed; "Student" was the *nom de plume* of the discoverer of this distribution, William Sealy Gosset

(continued on following page)

Topic	Discussion
System limits	Lines on a control chart displaced six standard deviations away from the average value; these lines will be exceeded by normal fluctuations only very rarely, so the organization can plan its work on the idea that the system limits will not be exceeded in a particular work unit
Underlying distribution	Data samples are acquired and analyzed so as to estimate the parameters of the distribution from which the samples arose; this distribution is called the underlying distribution
Uniform distribution	A distribution for which all outcomes are equally likely, as is found when flipping a coin or drawing a card from a deck
Variance	The sum of the squares of the differences among sample values and the average value; this definition applies to all distributions
Variate	A mathematical entity that takes on values according to a distribution, rule, or law
Weibull distribution	A distribution, attributed to Weibull, that is often used to model lifetime behavior, including bathtub-profile behavior and exponential lifetimes
Yield	The ratio of desired outcomes to all outcomes

Companion Web Site Content

This book is accompanied by a web site, www.ache.org/pubs/barry/start.cfm, that includes the lists of data required to work the cases to preclude the student having to rekey all of the data. The web site also contains sample spreadsheets showing the application of the statistical functions used in the book. A few of the cases are also worked in full on the web site to show the application of the method being taught.

The following will be found on the web site:

1. Data for all cases in Excel® format
2. Complete solutions for indicative cases
3. PowerPoint® templates for case reports
4. Complete analysis of examples not carried to completion in the text
5. A Microsoft Excel® "ice breaker"

About the Authors

Robert Barry, Ph.D., is a principal of Balester Consultants, a certified Six Sigma Master Black Belt, and a management consultant specializing in systems of extremely high reliability whose clients range from hospitals and utilities to the Alaska Pipeline. Dr. Barry holds a bachelor's degree from Iowa State University and master's and Ph.D. degrees from the University of Pittsburgh. He has completed executive management programs at the Harvard Business School and Harvard Law School. Dr. Barry holds 11 U.S. patents and has published widely on technical and management topics. He has held international senior management positions for Westinghouse, has served on the Penn State and University of Pittsburgh faculties, and is active in nonprofit organizations promoting the education and employment of people with severe physical and sensory handicaps.

Amy C. Murcko, APRN, is director of outcomes management and research at Sharon Regional Health System in Sharon, Pennsylvania. Ms. Murcko is a board-certified medical/surgical clinical nurse specialist with expertise in clinical performance improvement, project management, and case management. She is a certified Six Sigma Black Belt who holds a master's degree in medical/surgical nursing from Gannon University in Erie, Pennsylvania, and a bachelor's degree in nursing from the University of Pittsburgh. Ms. Murcko has worked in a variety of staff nurse, advanced practice, and management roles, and she is actively involved in emerging nursing and health policy issues through her work with the American Nurses Association.

Clifford E. Brubaker, Ph.D., is professor and dean of the School of Health and Rehabilitation Sciences at the University of Pittsburgh. He holds additional professorial appointments at the University of Pittsburgh in the departments of Neurological Surgery, Orthopedic Surgery, Industrial Engineering, and Bioengineering and with the McGowan Institute for Regenerative Medicine. Dr. Brubaker has contributed to research, education, and service in the fields of biomechanics, rehabilitation engineering, and assistive technology for more than 30 years. He received his bachelor's and master's degrees from Ball State University in Muncie, Indiana and his Ph.D. from the University of Oregon. Dr. Brubaker is past-president (1995–96) and Fellow of the Rehabilitation Engineering Society of North America and a Founding Fellow of the American Institute on Medical and Biological Engineering. He chaired the advisory committee that drafted the current long-range plan for the National Institute on Disability and Rehabilitation Research. Recently Dr. Brubaker was recognized by the *Pittsburgh Business Times* as the 2002 recipient of their Health Hero Award for Lifetime Achievement.